CW01215327

OPEN AND RELATIONAL THEOLOGY AND ITS SOCIAL AND POLITICAL IMPLICATIONS

MUSLIM AND CHRISTIAN PERSPECTIVES

JONATHAN J. FOSTER, MOUHANAD KHORCHIDE,
THOMAS JAY OORD, MANUEL SCHMID

SacraSage

Copyright © 2024 SacraSage Press

Graphic and design: Jonathan Foster, Nicole Sturk

All rights reserved. This book or any portion thereof may not be reproduced or used in any manner whatsoever without the express written permission of the publisher except for the use of brief quotations in a book review or scholarly journal.

NO AI TRAINING: Without in any way limiting the author [and publisher's] exclusive rights under copyright, any use of this publication to "train" generative artificial intelligence (AI) technologies to generate text is expressly prohibited. The author reserves all rights to license uses of this work for generative AI training and development of machine learning language models.

Print ISBN: 978-1-958670-12-5
Ebook ISBN: 978-1-958670-11-8

Printed in the United States of America Library of Congress Cataloguing-in-Publication Data

Open and Relational Theology and its Social and Political Implications: Muslim and Christian Perspectives

TABLE OF CONTENTS

Greetings from John B. Cobb, Jr. 1

Introduction Part I: Open and Relational Theology - *Thomas Jay Oord* 5

Introduction Part II: The Openness of God in Islam and Christianity: Communicative, social, and peace-promoting potentials of relational theology - *Manuel Schmid* 19

Process Relational Thought and Islam: Proposing a Novel Framework for Constructive Engagement with Modernity - *Jared Morningstar* 25

Ten Hopeful Ideas: In Conversation with Jared Morningstar - *Jay McDaniel* 45

Open and Relational Theology and its Social and Political Implications: Perspectives from Progressive Islam - *Adis Duderija* 51

The Responsibility of Embodying Godlike Attributes: In Conversation wth Adis Duderija - *Dave Andrews* 61

Nurturant Religion for a Better World - *John Sanders* 69

Nurturant and Authoritative Views of God: In Conversation with John Sanders - *Shabir Ally* 81

Birds with Wings Outspread: Christianity, Islam and the
Earth - *Catherine Keller* 89

Interreligious Open Theology and Human Exceptionalism:
In Conversation with Catherine Keller - *Johannes Grössl* 103

Iqbal's Process Relational Worldview: An Islamic Response
to Modern Challenges - *Saida Mirsadri*.........................109

Unforeseeable Possibilities: In Conversation with Saida
Mirsadri - *Michael Lodahl* 135

A Call for a United Faith Response to Our Current Climate
Crisis - *Greg Boyd* 145

The Social and Political Consequences of Open Theology.
An Islamic perspective - *Mouhanad Khorchide* 151

GREETINGS FROM JOHN B. COBB, JR.

JOHN B. COBB, Ph.D., founding co-director of the Center for Process Studies and Process & Faith, Professor Emeritus Claremont School of Theology, Visiting Professor at Vanderbilt, Harvard Divinity, and Chicago Divinity Schools. His writings include: *Christ in a Pluralistic Age; God and the World; For the Common Good and he is the* Co-winner of the Grawemeyer Award of Ideas Improving World Order.

Greetings to all of you. We people of the book have so much in common and yet do not often work together. Process thinking has been marginal in Christianity, but I had feared that it would be even more marginal in Islam. But now, I have been assured that the same possibilities exist there.

In Christianity, we have the advantage that the Hebrews, who produced most of our scriptures, thought in process terms. Events and stories are looked to for truth and guidance rather than substantial objects and their characteristics. I think the same is true for the Quran. I think for both, what has happened in history shapes our understanding of what we are now called to do in our unique historical situation.

Cultures that seek to find the meaning of life through past and present events have rarely attempted to systematize their metaphysics. This puts them at a disadvantage with thinkers in cultures that encourage such systematization. Greeks and Romans asked questions about Christian thought to which the Bible had no answers. Indeed, from a process perspective, they are the wrong questions. But because the Christians had not developed an explanation of why they were the wrong questions, their official teaching took the form of creeds formulated in terms of substances.

The idea that Christian faith is a matter of belief in creeds and the profoundly unbiblical affirmations the creeds convey have alienated us from other people of the book and even alienated Christians from their own book. I hope that working with Muslims, who are, I think, more fully tied to the book, will help us.

I am quite sure that Christian process theology is more congenial to the Bible than are the substance philosophies that have dominated our theologies. Would that Christians in the Roman Empire have been ready to critique the dominant philosophical ideas from a more Hebraic perspective! But even now, it is worth doing. In fact, as the dominance of substance thought with its inability to understand the central reality of relations is leading humanity to self-destruction, there has never been a greater need to recover the historically formed and oriented thinking associated with the book. In the book, there is no question about the importance of relations, physically, mentally, metaphysically, spiritually, and historically. There is no question that relations of cooperation are, and must be, more fundamental than relations of competition that so often end up in war.

We people of the book have much of which to repent. Fortunately, we have never denied that. Thankfully, we worship a merciful God. Our salvation is God's gift, not our achievement. But none of us suppose that simply admitting our failures and rejoicing in God's mercy is enough.

We are called to serve God in all dimensions, but most clearly in history. Even with the best intentions, we make mistakes and misinterpret what we are called to do. Despite our knowledge of the evils of idolatry, we absolutize ideas and loyalties that are less than God and less than the whole of God's creation. Perhaps we Christians have been the worst in this respect. We have absolutized our creeds in ways that have led us to see our fellow peoples of the book as evils to be destroyed. At least in this respect, Islam has been far better. In any case, if Christians and Muslims work together, we may help each other avoid idolatry. I think process thought can help.

There is increasing recognition that the human future is profoundly threatened by our continuing destruction of its natural base and our continuing favoring of violent competition over loving cooperation. Let us examine ourselves carefully and repent for all we do to support these global failures. But let us shout from the rooftops that God has shown us a better way, a way that even now could make a huge difference.

May this conference move us forward into unchartered waters. The changes that must occur are dangerous. They are not simple and comfortable. But they would give our grandchildren a chance. That is worth our paying some price. So may it be.

INTRODUCTION PART I:
Open and Relational Theology

THOMAS JAY OORD, Director of The Center for Open and Relational Theology (www.c4ort.com) and Director of the doctoral program in Open and Relational Theology at Northwind theological seminary (www.northwindseminary.org).

Open and relational theology is a wide umbrella of diverse ideas. It finds expression in various religions, concepts, traditions, beliefs, and intuitions. Despite this multiplicity, those under the open and relational umbrella affirm at least two important ideas:

- **Open** – God and creation experience moment by moment, and the future is open.
- **Relational** – All that exists gives and receives; God and creatures are relational.[1]

These ideas are central to what open and relational thinkers believe about who God is, how God acts, and the nature of creation. They fit our own experience because we naturally perceive life as open and relational. And these ideas find support in sacred scriptures.

---

[1]. For an accessible introduction to open and relational theology, see Thomas Jay Oord, *Open and Relational Theology: An Introduction to Life-Changing Ideas* (Grasmere, Id.: SacraSage, 2021).

Open and relational ideas stand at odds with many traditional theologies. Conventional ways of thinking characterize God as timeless, nonexperiential, static, nonrelational, distant, and unemotional. In this essay, I explain open and relational thinking—both core notions and other important ideas—and compare it to traditional approaches.

Relationality

Major figures in both Christianity and Islam deny God is relational.[2] They claim that creatures and creation do not affect or influence God. Ancient thinkers used the word "impassible" to describe the deity they believe is uninfluenced and unreceptive.

Many theologians also say God does not respond emotionally to creatures. Anselm, for instance, said God was compassionate only when considered from the human perspective, but not compassionate as God actually is.[3] After all, compassion involves being emotionally influenced by those who suffer, and an unemotional God cannot be influenced.

Open and relational theologians say God affects creation, and creation affects God.[4] God really suffers when we suffer and rejoices when we rejoice. Deity is passible. This view fits the witness of various scriptures, which portray God as interactive and emotionally engaged. God responds to what creatures do, sometimes feeling angry, sad, happy, or proud, depending on what creatures do.

---

2. For examples of Muslim theologians who deny divine possibility, see the writings of Al Ghazali and Averroes.

3. St. Anselm, *Proslogium*, Sidney Norton Deane, trans. (La Salle, IL, 1951), 13-14.

4. Among Muslims exploring open and relational theology, see contributors to this book and contributors to John Sanders and Klaus von Stosch, eds., *Divine Action: Challenges for Muslim and Christian Theology* (Paderborn: Brill, 2022); Farhan Shah, Open Horizons (https://www.openhorizons.org/farhan-shah.html). See also Michael Lodahl, *Claiming Abraham: Reading the Bible and the Qu'ran Side by Side* (Grand Rapids, Mich: Brazos, 2010).

Saying creatures affect God means the divine experience changes in response to others. This opposes another common idea among traditional theologians: that God is unchanging in all respects. The God whose experience is altered by what creatures do is obviously a God who changes. Most theologians say God is in all ways immutable; open and relational thinkers disagree.[5]

Some open and relational thinkers believe *all* creation influences God. They embrace panentheism.[6] Rather than thinking creation *is* divine or that creatures cannot make a difference to God, panentheists believe all creaturely actions affect God's moment-by-moment experience. All is *in* God's ongoing life, but the Creator is not identical to creation.

Open and relational thinkers often say God is in some respects passable and changing, but in other respects impassible and unchanging. Some call this "dipolar theism;" I call it God's essence-experience binate.[7] This view says God's eternal essence is unaffected and immutable. But creatures affect and change God's moment-by-moment experience. Some misunderstand open and relational theology as saying God has two natures. But the essence-experience binate identifies two aspects of what it means to be divine: God's essence and experience.

The advantages of affirming God's essence-experience binate are many. The binate allows theists to say God's nature of love never

---

5. Among the many open and relational theologians who reject absolute divine immutability, see Richard Swinburne, *The Coherence of Theism*, rev. ed., (Oxford: Oxford University Press, 1993).

6. Among the important books on panentheism, see Godehard Brüntrup, et. al., eds., *Panentheism and Panpsychism: Philosophy of Religion Meets Philosophy of Mind* (Mentis Verlag/Brill, 2020); Philip Clayton and Arthur Peacocke, eds., *In Whom We Live and Move and Have our Being* (Grand Rapids, Mich.: Eerdmans, 2004); Andrew Davis and Philip Clayton, *How I Found God in Everyone and Everywhere* (Monkfish, 2018).

7. For an accessible explanation of God's essence-experience binate, see Thomas Jay Oord, *Open and Relational Theology*, 102-03. Charles Hartshorne raised dipolar theism to prominence. See his essay "The Dipolar Conception of Deity," *Review of Metaphysics* 21:2 [1967], 273-89) and Donald Viney's explanation of it in "Hartshorne's Dipolar Theism and the Mystery of God" *Philosophia*, 35 (2007), 341-350.

changes, for instance, but God's giving-and-receiving love changes in response to creatures. God *always* loves, because it's God's immutable nature to do so, but God's love is perfectly sensitive to each situation, because God's experience is dynamic. The essence-experience binate allows the open and relational theologian to say God everlastingly knows all that's knowable, but the content of God's knowledge increases moment by moment. By essence, God is omniscient; by experience, God's knowledge grows.

God and Time

Theists have long pondered God's relation to time. Sacred scriptures of various traditions describe God acting timefully, in the sense of experiencing the forward flow of time. There are past moments of divine experience; God experiences in the present; and deity will experience in the future.

By contrast, traditional theologians say God is timeless. Augustine, for instance, claimed an essentially timeless God created time.[8] According to many, God's life is an eternal now with no duration. Scripture passages that say or imply God experiences time, repents, or responds to creatures are, according to traditional theologies, anthropomorphic projections.

Open and relational theologians believe God is an experiential and universal agent who experiences moment by moment.[9] Rather than nontemporal or "outside time," the open and relational God is pantemporal or "inside time."[10] The idea that a relational God in-

---

8. Augustine, *Confessions*, XI. xiii (16).
9. Alfred North Whitehead is a primary advocate for the ultimacy of time for God and creation. See his *Process and Reality: An Essay in Cosmology*, Corrected edition by David Ray Griffin and Donald W. Sherburne (New York: Free, 1978 [1929]). For an overview of Whitehead's view, see Daniel A. Dombrowski, *Whitehead's Religious Thought* (Albany, NY: SUNY, 2017).
10. Among the philosophically oriented works on God and time in open and relational thought, see David Basinger, *The Case for Freewill Theism: A Philosophical*

teracts with creation fits naturally with the idea God is passible and God's experience changes. The universal Spirit of love experiences giving-and-receiving relations.

Some traditional theologians argue God predestined everything from a timeless eternity. And many claim God exhaustively foreknows all that will occur. The problems with these claims are numerous. If God predestines and exhaustively foreknows all with certainty, the future must be settled and complete. But a settled and completed future is incompatible with free creaturely choosing among live options. God can't predestine or foreknow all if creatures freely choose among genuine possibilities.[11]

History is not like a prerecorded music album, say open and relational thinkers. It's more like an improvisational, in-the-moment jazz session, without predetermined outcomes.[12] Existence is an open-ended adventure rather than the unfolding of a pre-decided blueprint.[13] And rather than pre-programmed robots, at least complex

---

Assessment (Downers Grove, Ill.: 1996); Daniel A. Dombrowski, *Analytic Theism, Hartshorne, and the Concept of God* (Albany, NY: State University of New York Press, 1996); William Hasker, *God, Time, and Knowledge* (Ithaca, NY: Cornell University Press, 1989); R. T. Mullins, *The End of the Timeless God* (Oxford: Oxford University Press, 2016); Donald Wayne Viney, "God Only Knows? Hartshorne and the Mechanics of Omniscience" in *Hartshorne, Process Philosophy and Theology*, Robert Kane and Stephen Phillips, eds. (Albany, NY: State University of New York Press, 1989), 71–90; Keith Ward, *God, Chance, and Necessity* (Oxford: Oneworld, 1996); Nicholas Wolterstorff, "God Everlasting" in *Philosophy and Faith*, David Shatz, ed. (New York: McGraw, 2002), 62-69.

11. One of the more influential open and relational books addressing problems with predestination and foreknowledge is Clark H. Pinnock, et. al., *The Openness of God: A Biblical Challenge to the Traditional Understanding of God* (Downers Grove, Ill.: InterVarsity, 1994). See also Richard Rice, *The Future of Open Theism: Antecedents and Opportunities* (Downers Grove, IL: IVP Academic, 2020).

12. Jay McDaniel has often employed the jazz metaphor for open and relational theology. See articles in https://www.openhorizons.org

13. Gregory Boyd has criticized traditional theology as assuming a divine blueprint. Among Boyd's writings on this, see "Randomness and Assurance: Does Everything Happen for a Reason?" *The Other Journal* vol. 20 (https://theotherjournal.com/2012/02/randomness-and-assurance-does-everything-happen-for-a-reason).

creatures like humans have authentic say-so in their lives. God is on an adventure or playing in the jazz session. God has goals for creation's flourishing but does not control everyone or exert meticulous providence.[14]

Greek and Hebrew scriptures illustrate the main themes in open and relational theology. Passages that say God expresses regret and disappointment, for instance, suggest God is affected by what happens. God also feels badly about the foolish choices creatures make.[15] Open and relational ideas are exemplified when the writers of scripture portray God as surprised[16] or uncertain whether people will be faithful.[17] God sometimes has a change of mind and changes plans, often because of the prayers of the people.[18] God also lays out possibilities of what may or may not happen, depending on what creatures choose.[19]

That God is relational and the future open fit common views of petitionary prayer. When most people ask God to fix situations, provide wisdom, or heal, they hope God will respond. An impassible God cannot respond, however. And if the future is already settled, petitions for change make no sense. By contrast, open and relational theology affirms that our actions affect God, and the future is not yet

---

14. Bruce Epperly explores the open and relational idea of God and creation on an adventure in *Holy Adventure* (Nashville, Tenn.: Upper Room, 2008). Among the more influential open and relational theologies of providence, see Thomas Jay Oord, *The Uncontrolling Love of God* (Downers Grove, Ill.; IVP Academic, 2015); John Sanders, *The God Who Risks* (Downers Grove, Ill.: IVP, 2007).

15. E.g., Gen. 6:5–6; 1 Sam. 15:10, 35; Ezek. 22:29–31. Manuel Schmid criticizes open theists who claim the biblical text *perfectly* aligns with their position. The more sober claim is that scripture aligns better with open theism than alternative theologies. See Schmid, *God in Motion: A Critical Exploration of the Open Theism Debate* (Baylor University Press, 2021).

16. E.g., Isa. 5:3–7; Jer. 3:6-7; 19–20.

17. E.g., Gen. 22:12; Exod. 16:4; Deut. 8:2; 13:1–3; Judges 2:20–3:5; 2 Chron. 32:31.

18. E.g., Exod. 32:14; Num. 14:12–20; Deut. 9:13–14, 18–20, 25; 1 Sam. 2:27–36; 2 Kings 20:1–7; 1 Chron. 21:15; Jer. 26:19; Ezek. 20:5–22; Amos 7:1–6; Jonah 1:2; 3:2, 4–10.

19. E.g., Exod. 3:18–4:9; 13:17; Jer. 38:17–18, 20–21, 23; Ezek. 12:1–3.

determined. Consequently, prayers influence God and creation, and the future will be different, at least in some way, when we pray.[20]

God's Power

Some traditional theologies say God exerts all power, entirely determining all that occurs. In them, creaturely freedom is an illusion. Others say creatures are free, but in some mysterious way, God controls all. This makes little to no sense, however; God can't control all, but creatures exert self-control. Our experience of free choices does not align with such theologies.

Open and relational thinkers reject the idea that God controls all. They believe a loving God does not fully determine everything but empowers creatures to make free choices. In philosophical circles, this view is called "libertarian free-will." Open and relational thinkers don't believe creaturely freedom is unlimited, however. We choose in contexts, among relations, in response to limitations, and from relevant options. Even God's freedom is limited, at least by what is logical and the divine nature.[21]

Open and relational thinkers differ among themselves regarding God's power. They all say humans express freedom and God does not always control, but they disagree about whether and if God *ever* determines outcomes singlehandedly. Some say God voluntarily self-limits and *rarely* controls. Others say the metaphysical laws of existence prevent God from controlling. Still, others say uncontrolling love comes first in God's nature, and because God always loves, God never

---

20. Among open and relational book addressing prayer, see Bruce Epperly, *Praying with Process Theology (*River Lane, 2017); Mark Karris, *Divine Echoes* (Nashville, Tenn.: Quoir, 2018); Marjorie Suchocki, *In God's Presence* (St. Louis, Mo.: Chalice, 1996).

21. Thomas Jay Oord explores the limits of God's power in *The Death of Omnipotence and Birth of Amipotence* (Grasmere, Id: SacraSage, 2023).

controls. Some open and relational thinkers reject divine omnipotence; others affirm qualified omnipotence.[22]

The various views of God's power lead to diverse perspectives on God's creating, miracles, and ability to bring about ultimate victory. Some open and relational thinkers affirm the view that emerged in the 3rd century that God created the universe from absolutely nothing (*creatio ex nihilo*). Others affirm that God creates from creation.[23] Some claim God occasionally interrupts the creation's causal chains to do miracles. Others say miracles occur only when creatures cooperate with God, or the conditions of creation are conducive. Some claim God can use omnipotent power to bring about the ultimate fulfillment of creation. Others say creation's fulfillment only comes through God's uncontrolling love and creaturely cooperation.

Perhaps the best known advantage of saying God cannot control is that it solves the problem of evil.[24] All open and relational thinkers say a loving God does not cause evil. Creatures cause evil when they purposely hurt one another or when they injure by accident. But those open and relational thinkers who reject omnipotence say God *cannot* singlehandedly prevent the evil that others do. Consequently, a non-omnipotent God is not morally responsible for hurt and harm. The

---

22. See Oord, *The Death of Omnipotence and Birth of Amipotence*. Jonathan Foster portrays controlling power as "Omnipotence" with a capital O in *Theology of Consent: Mimetic Theory in an Open and Relational Universe* (Grasmere, Id.: SacraSage, 2022). Anna Case-Winters rejects omnipotence in *God's Power: Traditional Understandings and Contemporary Challenges* (Louisville, Ky.: Westminster/John Knox, 1990). John Sanders argues for qualified omnipotence in *The God Who Risks*.
23. See Catherine Keller's criticism of *creatio ex nihilo* in *The Face of the Deep* (New York: Routledge, 2003). For an edited collection of open and relational essays in support and opposition to creation from nothing, see Thomas Jay Oord, ed., *Theologies of Creation: Creatio ex Nihilo and Its New Rivals* (New York: Routledge, 2012).
24. David Ray Griffin has been a central voice for rejecting omnipotence and solving the central plank in the problem of evil. See his ground-breaking book, *God, Power, and Evil: A Process Theodicy* (Louisville, KY: Westminster John Knox, 2004). For a more accessible solution to evil, see Thomas Jay Oord, *God Can't: How to Believe in God and Love after Tragedy, Abuse, and Suffering* (Grasmere, Id.: SacraSage, 2019).

inability to prevent evil singlehandedly includes not being able to stop the unnecessary suffering we witness among other animals and all of creation.[25]

To say God gives freedom and agency to creation points to a key idea in open and relational theology: creatures can partner with their Creator. This partnership means creatures play a role in deciding what occurs moment by moment.[26] The God-world relationship makes a real difference to the emerging history of existence.[27]

When creatures play a role in deciding reality, they can rightly be considered valuable. Traditional theologies that say God alone decides history do not support creaturely significance. In them, creatures don't *really* matter. And when salvation is thought to be decided by God alone, creatures are mere pawns moved by the divine chess master. Open and relational thinkers, by contrast, argue that salvation is a symbiotic or synergistic process whereby God acts first and invites creaturely response. The decisions creatures make play a part in redemption.

Some open and relational thinker point to the Trinity as the best example of noncoercive partnership. The dance among divine members, say many, should be emulated by creatures. Others reject the Trinity and point to God's everlasting relationship with creation as the

---

25. Bethany Sollereder addresses animal suffering and God's love in *God, Evolution, and Animal Suffering: Theodicy without a Fall* (New York: Routledge, 2020). Ilia Delio addresses love and evolution in *The Unbearable Wholeness of Being* (Maryknoll, NY: Orbis, 2013).
26. For a collection of open and relational theology essay exploring partnership with God, see Timothy Reddish, et. al., eds. *Partnering with God: Exploring Collaboration in Open and Relational Theology* (Grasmere, Id.: SacraSage, 2021).
27. For helpful books on the God-world relationship, see Joseph Bracken, *Reciprocal Causality in an Event-Filled World* (London: Lexington, 2022); Philip Clayton, *Adventures in Spirit* (Minneapolis: Fortress, 2008); John B. Cobb, Jr., *God and the World* (Philadelphia: Westminster, 1965); Nancy R. Howell, *A Feminist Cosmology* (Humanities Press, 2000); Michael Lodahl, *God of Nature and of Grace: Reading the World in a Wesleyan Way* (Nashville: Abingdon, 2003).

model of collaboration.[28] Divine love for creation reveals God's everlasting and uncontrolling love, what we might call "essential *hesed*."[29] Still, others reject both the Trinity and the idea God everlastingly relates with creation.[30]

The Role of Experience

Because creatures play an essential role in history, open and relational theologies take creaturely experience seriously. The importance of experience for theology is a common theme among contemporary scholarship and both modern and postmodern theology. The seriousness with which open and relational thinkers take creaturely experience is evident in various ways.

Open and relational thinkers have been at the fore of the science-and-religion dialogue, for instance. They take seriously recent research on relationships in psychology, sociology, and medicine, and they believe such sciences help us discern what God's relationships might be like. Open and relational theology also fits the views of existence found among physicists, biologists, and chemists. An evolving and expanding creation naturally aligns with a vision of God as evolving, expanding, and continually creating.[31]

---

28. For more on the advantages and disadvantages of affirming the Trinity, see Karen Baker-Fletcher, *Dancing with God* (St. Louis, Mo.: Chalice, 2006); Dale Tuggy, *What is the Trinity?* (Createspace, 2017); Keith Ward, *Christ and Cosmos* (Cambridge: Cambridge University Press, 2015).
29. Thomas Jay Oord explains and argues for essential *hesed* in *Pluriform Love: An Open and Relational Theology of Well-Being* (Grasmere, Id.: SacraSage, 2022).
30. I suspect most Muslim theologians affirm this perspective. But you will find it among Christian open and relational Unitarians like Dale Tuggy.
31. Among open and relational thinkers who have made significant contributions to the science-and-religion dialogue, see John Polkinghorne, *From Physicist to Priest, an Autobiography* (London: SPCK, 2007); Ian Barbour, *Nature, Human Nature, and God* (Minneapolis: Fortress, 2002); Philip Clayton, *God and Contemporary Science* (Edinburgh: Edinburgh University Press, 1997); Ilia Delio, *Christ in Evolution* (Orbis, 2011).

More humans identify as female than as male or nonbinary. And yet traditional theologies often dismiss or discount female experience. Many women find open and relational theology helpful for how it validates their experiences, especially the profoundly relational dimensions of power.[32] Other minority voices and nonbinary people find in open and relational thinking a way to account for their experiences. The God who cannot control does not endorse the colonization of peoples or oppression of minority peoples.[33]

Religious experiences and traditions are diverse, because the wisdom in them is also diverse. Open and relational theology accounts for this variety by acknowledging the multifarious histories of people and ideas. And because this theological approach says God self-reveals in diverse but uncontrolling ways, various claims about ultimate reality among the world's major religions make sense in an open and relational framework.[34]

Because open and relational thinking sees existence as interrelated, many in the open and relational community have been at the fore of calling for ecological and political reform.[35] After all, no one is an island. And good theology accounts for the social dimensions of

---

[32] One of the best overall introductions to and analysis of feminism is by process scholars. See Monica A. Coleman, Nancy R. Howell, and Helene Talon Russell, eds., *Creating Women's Theology* (Eugene, Or.: Pickwick, 2011). See also Karen Winslow, *Imagining Equity* (Nashville, Tenn.: Wesley's Foundery, 2021).

[33] See Ekaputra Tupamahu, "A Decolonial View of God," in *Uncontrolling Love*, Lisa Michaels, et. al., eds (Grasmere, Id.: SacraSage, 2017); Randy S. Woodley, *Indigenous Theology and the Western Worldview* (Grand Rapids, Mich.: Baker, 2022).

[34] Among the books addressing religious pluralism from an open and relational perspective, see Bruce Epperly, *The Elephant is Running: Process and Open and Relational Theologies and Religious Pluralism* (Grasmere, Id.: SacraSage, 2022); David Ray Griffin, *Deep Religious Pluralism* (Nashville, Tenn.: John Knox, 2005); Jay McDaniel, *Ghandi's Hope* (New York: Orbis, 2005); Marjorie Suchocki, *Divinity and Diversity* (Nashville, Tenn.: Abingdon, 2003).

[35] See, for instance, Greg Boyd, *The Myth of a Christian Nation* (Grand Rapids, Mich.: Zondervan, 2005); Bruce Epperly, *Process Theology and Politics* (Energion, 2020); Catherine Keller, *Facing Apocalypse* (New York: Orbis, 2021); Philip Clayton and Wm Andrew Schwartz, *What is Ecological Civilization?* (Process Century, 2019).

reality. On a planet headed for ecological destruction, prophetic voices call for visions that promote social and planetary well-being. In fact, essays in this book break new ground in this regard.

Love

To close this introduction to major themes in open and relational theology, I point to love. Love is a relational activity that seeks greater values. Or, as I define it, love acts intentionally, in relational response to God and others, to promote overall well-being.[36] Because open and relational theology affirms values, creaturely freedom, and relationality for God and creation, it provides an ideal framework for theologies of love.

Traditional theologies often neglect or distort love, especially divine love. Many deny that God is relational, for instance, which makes accounting for the relational dimensions of God's love impossible. Others claim God sends people to eternal conscious torment in hell, which strikes most people as incompatible with forgiving love. Some claim God only loves the elect, which means divine love is limited rather than universal. Others say God loves only the most valuable, and because God is most valuable, God only loves Godself. Still, others say God causes or allows genuine evil, which opposes our deepest intuition of what love does. Traditional theologies rarely align with our intuitions about and experiences of love.[37]

The open and relational philosopher Charles Hartshorne summarizes his thought with these words: "My ultimate intuitive clue in

---

36. In *Pluriform Love*, I explain this definition of love and defend it in the face of major Christian theologies.

37. Among the open and relational thinkers who criticize traditional views of divine love and offer alternatives, see David Polk, *God of Empowering Love* (Anoka, Mn.: Process Century, 2016); Catherine Keller, *On the Mystery* (Minneapolis: Fortress, 2008), Oord, *Pluriform Love*; Paul Sponheim, *Love's Availing Power* (Minneapolis: Fortress, 2011); Daniel Day Williams, *The Spirit and the Forms of Love* (New York: Harper & Row, 1968).

philosophy is that 'God is love'." And "God is definable as that of the being worthy to be loved with all one's heart, mind, soul, and entire being."[38] Thomas Jay Oord argues that "open and relational thought provides the best overall framework for understanding and promoting love."[39]

John Sanders offers an open and relational argument for a loving God as nurturing. Sanders contrasts the God who nurtures with the authoritarian God who controls and the permissive God who is unengaged. Research shows that children whose parents neglect or try to control them fare far worse than the children of parents who nurture them. Analogously, the open and relational God of love promotes the good of creation by persuading rather than manipulating, empowering rather than abandoning, and inspiring rather that standing aloof.[40] Open and relational theology portrays God as nurturing.

Those who love and care about the well-being of the world are wise to embrace an open and relational vision. Enhancing human civilization, the planet and her diverse creatures, and even God's own experience, makes sense in an open and relational theological framework. The essays in this book explore this theme.

---

38. Charles Hartshorne, *The Philosophy of Charles Hartshorne*, Lewis Edwin Hahn, ed. (La Salle, Ill: Open Court, 1991), 700.
39. Oord, *Open and Relational Theology*, 117. See also *Pluriform Love*.
40. John Sanders explores the consequences of thinking God is authoritarian or nurturant in *Embracing Prodigals* (Eugene, Or.: Wipf and Stock, 2020).

INTRODUCTION PART II:
The Openness of God in Islam and Christianity: Communicative, social, and peace-promoting potentials of relational theology

MANUEL SCHMID, Theologian of the Reformed Church Zurich, Head of the Digital Laboratory "RefLab." For more information, see www.reflab.ch.

This volume brings together contributions from Islamic and Christian theologians presented at the December 2022 online conference "Open and Relational Theology and its Social and Political Implications." The conference and this book explore backgrounds, possibilities, and starting points for developing an open and relational theology based on Quranic and biblical grounds.

Open theism, a fundamental element of open and relational theology, is close in content to process theology and to the philosophy of freedom of German idealism. Open theism develops a dynamic, interactive view of the relationship between God and the world in opposition to deterministic views. At many points, it also touches upon progressive Islamic theology, which distances itself from static conceptions of God and controlling omnipotence and instead opts for a salvific mobility of God.

Keeping these concepts in mind helps us renew our ability to speak religiously in a modern society, but beyond that, also to promote an understanding of religion that strengthens the human being as a responsible actor and, through an ethos of love and mercy, release peace-making and creation-preserving potentials.

Some of the Christian contributors are among the most important representatives of "open theism" (Gregory Boyd and John Sanders); others are prominent thinkers and representatives of process theology (John Cobb, Catherine Keller, Jay McDaniel, and Tom Oord), and others belong under the broader umbrella of relational theology (Michael Lodahl, Johannes Grössl, Aaron Langenfeld, Dave Andrews).

The Islamic perspective is represented, as well, by weighty pioneers of its field. They stand for progressive forms of Islam and argue from a process-theological, relational, panentheistic image of God (Jared Morningstar and Adis Duderija). A perspective from the history of theology is represented by Saida Mirsadri, who draws attention to the contemporary theological potentials of Muhammad Iqbal's relational process worldview.

It is also worth emphasizing that many contributions in this volume do not stop at the internal religious perspective of their authors but explicitly take an interreligious standpoint as well. Thus, for example, John Cobb pleads for a cooperation of the "peoples of the book," Gregory Boyd longs for a "united faith response to our current climate crisis," and Catherine Keller unfolds a vision of the world religions as "earth religions" (i.e., as communities that draw a planetary consciousness and responsibility from their faith.) This interreligious volume is in the spirit of these concerns and represents a unique initiative in Christian and Islamic theology.

In the following, I draw some lines of thought in order to indicate the direction in which the contributions of this volume move—and in which it is also worthwhile to reflect beyond the impulses of this book.

1 Sources: Traces in the Holy Scriptures and their Interpretative traditions

This book is oriented under the umbrella term of open and relational theology as coined by Thomas Jay Oord. The "open" portion of open and relational theology—the idea that the future is yet settled—is an important, if not controversial, concept within the US-American evangelical world in recent years.

For biblical and philosophical reasons, open theists lobby for a renewal of classic Christian theology, where the interrelational dynamic between God and man is seriously considered, and God is discovered as a participant in his creation's history. According to open-theistic conviction, God moves towards a still undetermined (open) future, which will only be determined in interaction with his creation.

Open theologians cite the God of the Bible who grieves, changes his mind, repents, displays disappointment, and a willingness to learn to emphasize that Scripture contains a theology of freedom and relationality. The history of Christian theology offers numerous examples of thinkers who have been opposed to the deterministic tendencies of classical theology and who advocated a more relational and interactive version of the God-world relationship (e.g., Charles Hartshorne, Hans Urs von Balthasar, and Jürgen Moltmann).

Such efforts are now also found in Islamic theology, both in its contemporary approach of re-reading the Quran from the perspective of modern philosophy of freedom and its importance on God's relational interest and human empowerment to shape life.

Islamic scholars have made decisive contributions to the recontextualization and inculturation of Islam under modern conditions (e.g., Zachria Ibrahim, more recently Mouhanad Khorchide, Muna Tatari, and Darius Asghar-Zadeh). They reference passages in their Holy Scriptures, namely to Quranic testimonies of God's dynamic and responsive interaction with man, but also to far-reaching traditions of interpretation in Islamic history.

The traditions of the Mu'tazilites, an important rationalistic-philosophical school of Islam dating back to Wasil Ibn' Ata in the 8th century, are particularly fruitful here. This movement experienced its heyday from the late 9th to the mid-11th century. During this period, the Mu'tazilites played a decisive role in Islamic thought by focusing on God's justice towards man. Given that judgment can only be called just when referring to free, non-determined acts, the Mu'tazilite tradition found that the free self-determination of man is fundamental.

God's omnipotence and omniscience are also redefined in this way because a God who respects the freedom of his creatures does not unilaterally determine the course of history. This is a God who leaves the future open for the realization of human decisions.

2 Guiding Principles: Love and mercy as the key characteristics of God

While the theological approach of the Mu'tazilites was strongly based on the commitment to God's justice, contemporary Islamic theologians such as Mouhanad Khorchide or the Muslim scholar Muna Tatari focus primarily on God's mercy as the fundamental paradigm. According to the dictum "Islam is mercy," a theology of empowerment and liberation of the human being for the sake of love is unfolding. Based on the recurrent Qur'anic confession of God's mercy and love towards humans, God is understood as the loving Creator who wants to invite his creatures into a transcendent relationship.

This approach to Islamic theology resonates with the openness we find in Old Testament texts that speak to God's mobility, interaction, readiness to engage with man, willingness to be disappointed or rejected by man, and then to pursue him again and again. These are all understood to be evidence of God's love.

If this is true, then the attributes of God, which are crucially important to Christianity and Islam, can be reconsidered. For example, God's omnipotence should be considered in light of his love and mercy, not as an all-controlling providence or an uncompromising assertion of power. When omnipotence is considered in this way, we see it as a power that empowers others, sets others free, and pursues goals both in cooperation with man and the world.

The omniscience of God, in turn, does not necessarily go along with a complete and definitive foreknowledge of the future; rather, as God knowing the fullness of what can be known at any given time. The past up to the present is a definite course of events, but the future as unrealized possibility, which is realized in the course of the common history of God and man.

Also, the classical confession of the immutability of God can be modified. God's unchangeable love and mercy means he is distinctly changeable, for he is always ready to respond to current circumstances and to interact with his creatures. In other words, God's changeability in his actions is a consequence of his unchangeability in nature and will.

3 Potentials: Chances of an open theology for religion and society

Both open theism and those reframing Islamic theology are motivated by the desire to bring language and understanding about the faith into present real life. Both Christian and Islamic communities want to meet the question of how, especially in 21st-century Western society, we can talk about God in a way that has sociopolitical, diaconal, and peace-promoting implications. A theology of God's relationality and openness provides numerous starting points.

On the one hand, open theology wants to emphasize the importance of man before God; for God to take him seriously as a partner to act and co-create. For God is with man in the vicissitudes and imponderables of life, leading with patience and flexible love toward the future. We are in a moment in history when such an interactive version of the God-human relationship makes great sense.

On the other hand, open theology wants to emphasize in a special way the responsibility of man in relation to God, to fellow man, and to the environment. Man is an influential actor in the structure of this creation and the preservation of the environment, the continued existence and peaceful coexistence of mankind. Within the context of open theology, there is no guaranteed divine providence to look to for help; rather, there are concrete, salvific intentions that God wants to realize in interaction with human beings, and for which individual human beings and religious communities share responsibility.

Open and relational theology thus becomes a promising, fresh way to approach both the Biblical and Qur'anic texts and the theology of Christianity and Islam. In pursuing this way, we hope to gain a religious language that connects to our modern society and contributes to the common good.

PROCESS RELATIONAL THOUGHT AND ISLAM:
Proposing a Novel Framework for Constructive Engagement with Modernity

JARED MORNINGSTAR, Communications Director, Center for Process Studies and Operations Assistant, Cobb Institute. For more information, see https://jaredmorningstar.com.

———

One of the major challenges for contemporary Islamic intellectual projects is creatively engaging the nebulous and elusive concept of "modernity." The various modern ideas that loom large in the consciousness of contemporary Muslims—such as the rights of women, the ideals of liberalism, the institution of the nation-state, the structures of global capitalism, the scientific method and technological advancement, and secularism—are all in relationship, one way or another, to this meta-concept of modernity. As such, developing a robust, dynamic, and flexible framework for approaching modernity in its various aspects is necessary if Islamic engagement with these ideas is going to be more than a set of disconnected endeavors and reactive postures lacking a cohesive basis.

To date, a significant portion of Muslim thinkers have tended to approach modernity with frameworks that either lead to a wholesale rejection of much of what is perceived as modern or a broad adoption of the sensibilities of Western modernity. Both these responses leave something to be desired, as they lack a critical orientation to their own methodologies and presuppositions, whether traditionally-grounded or adapted from modern Western sources. Instead of simply reproducing either pre-modern traditions or an exogenous Western modernity—moves which invariably lead to harmful forms of reductionism—I propose a *bi-directional* critical movement between tradition and modernity so that a creative synthesis may be achieved; a synthesis that avoids the trappings of both a naïve traditionalism which refuses to incorporate historical or contextualist thinking or a crude modernism which is blind to the integrity of a tradition and is careless in trying to import supposedly superior foreign intellectual material. To this end, process-relational philosophy may provide instructive resources. On the one hand, process thought undercuts and transforms many of the foundational epistemological and metaphysical ideas at the heart of modernity from thinkers such as Kant and Descartes, while on the other hand, it maintains appreciation of the value and insights of religious traditions in a way that avoids decadent romanticism by considering such matters as always in development and inseparable from context. These features of process-relational thought allow Muslim intellectuals to deconstruct dysfunctional ideas from both Western modernity and Islamic traditions while encouraging the creative *reconstruction* and *synthesis* of material from both of these spheres, leading to more holistic and dynamic responses to the challenges of contemporary times.

It will be helpful to outline existing Islamic responses to modernity to begin. One popular scheme in this regard is a threefold division of modernists, puritanical reformists, and traditionalists.[1] Muslim mod-

---

1. See Joseph Lumbard, "The Decline of Knowledge and the Rise of Ideology in the Modern Islamic World" in Lumbard (editor), *Islam, Fundamentalism, and the Betrayal of Tradition: Essays by Western Muslim Scholars, Revised and Expanded Edition* (Bloomington, Ind.: World Wisdom, 2009) for a clear articulation of this three-fold division. This framework is widely employed by self-identified traditional voices within the field of Islamic studies, especially in the niches of Sufi studies, Islamic mystical traditions, and Islamic theology.

ernists are those inspired by Western intellectual achievements, particularly in social and scientific domains, and those who seek to replicate this form of perceived progress in Islamic societies. They draw upon modern Western philosophy and culture to self-consciously modify, qualify, and augment Islamic thinking and living in hopes of moving towards a more adaptive, dynamic, and rich form of Islam that may more effectively navigate unique modern challenges and possibilities.

The puritanical reformists have the opposite orientation and point to the perceived moral degradation and irreligiosity of the modern West, insisting a return to "pure" tradition is the proper response. Here the focus becomes the sufficiency of the material provided directly by the Qur'an and the Sunnah, with partisans of this camp claiming that the supposedly univocal guidance of Revelation, interpreted in light of the sayings and actions example of the Prophet (ﷺ), holds the keys to certainty and moral uprightness which modernity disrupts. These values are evident in proclamations from a major reformist voice such as Sayyid Qutb. In *Milestones,* he writes that "it is necessary to revive that Muslim community which is buried under the debris of the man-made traditions of several generations, and which is crushed under the weight of those false laws and customs which are not even remotely related to the Islamic teachings."[2] And further: "The main reason for the difference between the first unique and distinguished group of Muslims and later Muslims is that the purity of the first source of Islamic guidance was mixed with various other sources."[3] Here one sees both the distaste for "man-made traditions"—whether they be classical Islamic traditions or those from the modern West—which are considered the source of the dysfunctions contemporary Muslims are

---

2. Sayyid Qutb, *Milestones* (New Delhi: Abdus Sami, 2002), *9.*
3. Ibid., 17.

experiencing, as well as the claim that a return to just the pure sources of the religion is the solution to these dysfunctions.[4]

The traditionalists are distinguished from both the modernists and the puritanical reformists by a greater degree of fidelity to classic traditions of law, theology, and spirituality, seeing these as offering refuge from the fragmentation and decadence of modernity. Here, deep contact and continuity with the inherent richness, dynamism, and breadth of traditional Islamic thought is the answer to the disruptions of modernity. Fuad Naeem describes this position on theological grounds: "One of the Names of God in Islam is *al-Ḥaqq*, the Truth. In light of this, the Islamic intellectual and spiritual tradition has always emphasized the primacy of truth, wherever it may be found, for all divergent truths are unified in and testify ultimately to the one Truth, God. This is why Islam does not need to be reformed or modernized; it already contains within itself the principles necessary for renewal from within. These principles provide the discernment to both integrate truth wherever it is found and to reject falsehood decisively."[5]

From this perspective, the Islamic tradition is already sufficiently equipped to grapple with modernity due to the historical preoccupation of Muslims with truth as a means to be in relationship with the Divine. This truth-seeking disposition is especially clear in the case of Sufism, where the goal is experiential knowledge of God, but may also be identified in historical phenomena such as Muslim appropriation of Greek philosophical systems and the zest for scientific exploration of Muslims in the classical era. As such, traditionalists maintain that the repository of philosophical schemas and dynamic methodologies that is the Islamic intellectual tradition at large contains all that is

---

4. Qutb proclaims this quite explicitly: "We must return to that pure source from which [the Salaf] derived their guidance, the source which is free from any mixing or pollution" Ibid., 21-22.

5. Fuad Naeem, "A Traditional Islamic Response to the Rise of Modernism" in *Islam, Fundamentalism, and the Betrayal of Tradition*, 111.

necessary to address modern questions—the issue at hand isn't navigating unique challenges of modernity so much as maintaining contact with the richness of the classical traditions. The traditionalists call their coreligionists to return with confidence to their own expansive intellectual heritage rather than becoming distracted by the prowess of Western science and philosophy or retreating into a more reactive posture of narrow scripturalism. Hence Lumbard's contention that "puritanical reformists [abandon the principles of traditional Islamic thought] because they favor an opaque literalism which denies the efficacy of our speculative, intuitive, and imaginal faculties. Modernists do so because they have capitulated to the mental habits of their conquerors, conditioned as they are by relativism, scientism, and secular humanism. Each side continues to advance its position, but there is no dialogue; for in the absence of the traditional Islamic modes of interpretation, there is no basis for a common discourse among Muslims."[6]

This typology, employed by Lumbard et al. in *Islam, Fundamentalism, and the Betrayal of Tradition*, offers a helpful general sketch, but if it is reified, it can become misleading. Indeed, the boundaries between these responses are porous, and there are areas of allegiance where two camps will come together on certain questions. While Lumbard and his coauthors in the volume seek to promote the perspective of traditionalism as the most capable framework for dynamically responding to the problems of modernity, I contend that there are under-examined tensions within this camp that require serious attention before traditionalism may become truly effective in providing navigation through modernity and beyond. This "big tent" style traditionalism, which typically identifies itself with the whole gamut of Islamic orthodoxy from Akbarian Sufism to the Hanbali school of law, lacks mechanisms for internal discernment and self-critique that are necessary as various factions within classical Islam attempt to

---

6. Lumbard, *Islam, Fundamentalism, and the Betrayal of Tradition*, 41.

put forth their own perspectives on modernity and the various particular issues it raises as "the traditional perspective." Lumbard himself can be placed in the lineage of the aptly-named "Traditionalist school" who—following Seyyed Hossein Nasr and other pioneers in this perspective—take the mystical metaphysics of Sufi intellectual traditions as the most authoritative articulation of Islam. But while philosophical Sufism may provide a dynamic and flexible framework for addressing contemporary questions, if traditionalists of this variety are unwilling to criticize not only the puritanical reformists and modernists who they see as breaking strongly from classical methodologies, but also their fellow traditionalists whose legal and theological thinking has ossified, then their project of responding more holistically to modernity will be continually frustrated.[7]

The late Shahab Ahmed, in his magisterial work *What is Islam? The Importance of Being Islamic*, critiques a whole range of analytical frameworks employed to understand the object-phenomenon of Islam. Ahmed contends that an essential, definitive feature of Islam is *internal contradiction*. Any analytic framework which attempts to

---

7. The vagueness and many potential signifiers of the term "traditionalist" is core to the weakness of this analytical framework. "The Traditionalist school," whose lineage traces itself back to European esoteric philosophers and converts to Islam such as René Guénon and Frithjof Schuon, provides a very different sense of the definitive core of tradition compared to those who identify with "traditionalism" in a more general sense. The former is much more focused on the mystical, metaphysical dimensions of Islam as holding epistemological supremacy, whereas the latter likely takes juridical traditions and dominant schools of *'aqīdah* as primarily constitutive of normative Islam. Those adhering to the perspective of the aforementioned Traditionalist school maintain that there is in fact no genuine conflict between mystical perspectives and the normativities of *fiqh* and *'aqīdah*, yet it is not at all difficult to locate examples in Islamic history where legal and theological orthodoxies come into conflict with perspectives grounded in mystical or metaphysical normativities. While the extent and scale of this conflict has been highly exaggerated and reified in much Orientalist scholarship, those championing the cohesiveness and analytical usefulness of the category of "tradition" have in many cases simply produced an inverse exaggeration, with the result being a blindness towards endogenous tensions and competing normativities in Islam which leave those employing this framework ill equipped to navigate inherent internal complexities.

approach the study of Islam which cannot deal with this empirical fact—as seen through, for example, the incommensurable visions of Islamic normativity presented by the doctors of law on the one hand and certain Sufi poets and Islamic philosophers on the other hand[8]— is fundamentally ill-equipped to properly characterize Islam. In this respect, traditionalism clearly fails, as the framework espouses an essential unity of Islam, wherein legal, theological, and mystical traditions are theorized as each having its own niche, which together form a complex, interdependent system where every part has an essential, irreducible function in relation to the whole.

While this vision is very evocative and compelling in its aesthetics of harmony, historically and empirically, it leaves something to be desired. An ecological metaphor may help to further elucidate this point. Here, we can view Islam as a complex ecosystem, with the individual sciences of law, theology, and Sufism seen as particular organisms. This helps to further highlight phenomena such as dynamics of "predation" where the competition between political, spiritual, and legal authorities influences the development of orthodoxies in contentious and historically-contingent ways. Here one also clearly sees periods of rupture and great change where previous relations which constituted patterns of homeostasis are thrown into question, such as in the case

---

8. In the first chapter of this magisterial study, "Six Questions about Islam," Ahmed highlights what he sees as six prototypical examples of Islam's internal contradictions. He explores material from the Islamic philosophers, Sufism, traditions of visual art, and courtly wine-drinking customs, showing that in all of these cases, the relevant agents considered themselves to be involved in something particularly *Islamic*, even as many of these acts and frameworks of intelligibility presented a form of Islamic normativity that contrasts and conflicts with juridical and scripturalist perspectives which are so often taken as most definitive of Islam. Ahmed is not reproducing Orientalist perspectives which, in noting many of the same tensions and contradictions, try to explain Sufism, Islamic art, etc. as extra-Islamic traditions competing with the *real* Islam which is defined by legal and scriptural core, but rather that the claims to Islam of these alternative Islamic normativities must be taken just as seriously by the analyst as the legalist claims, particularly as the norms of the Sufi-philosophical amalgam were so diffuse in the Bengal-to-Balkans complex that represents the majority of historical Islam.

of the Islamic encounter with Greek thought and the transformations which ensued in Islamic intellectual life as philosophers and theologians began critically appropriating, transforming, and deconstructing this material. In any case, viewed ecologically, tradition is not seen as a pre-ordained harmony of various perspectives in different domains, but a complex web of contingent and complex relations constantly in processes of change and evolution.

The benefit of this ecological perspective is further demonstrated when it comes to considering specific constitutive elements of Islamic orthodoxies. As evolutionary biologists will contend, the "fittedness" of the component organisms within any ecosystem is not an inherent trait but something wholly relational between the organism, the other organisms with which it is in relation, and the larger environment in which the organism finds itself. As such, a trait that allows something to exist as an indispensable, harmonious component of a system within one context will find itself ill-adapted to contribute productively in a different state of its system. The inability of the traditionalist perspective to perceive the existing fault lines within tradition itself leaves the framework susceptible to a reification of the particular *features* or *content* of Islamic intellectual traditions as essentially constitutive of a harmonious, dynamic, and adaptable system rather than conceptualizing this holistic state developing as a result of *relational* factors between the elements *and* between a broader environment. This failure only becomes more acute in contexts of significant disruption, as is the encounter with modernity. Even if it is the case that some exact combination of features constituted a holistic harmony between law, theology, spirituality, art, poetry, ethics, etc., in the classical period, it does not follow that reproducing the same features in the contemporary context will reproduce the same state of harmony and dynamism—the context has shifted and colored the relations between elements in particular ways so that homeostasis and dynamic agency need be achieved via new relational arrangements.

For example, Ahmed, following Talal Asad, identifies *law* as a quintessential feature of modernity and of its prototypical political unit, the nation-state.

> *Law* is a *leitmotif* of the *modern* human condition in a manner and degree unprecedented in any prior period of history. Not only is the fundamental organizational unit of modern human society to which all human subjects *belong*—that is, the nation state—*constituted* as a *legally-determined* entity (as distinct from a divinely- or patrimonially-determined entity)—one might even say that the nation-state is a legal fiction: it is, literally, *made up* by law—but the modern human condition is more thoroughly pervaded by the technology and force of the structures of law than has been any other human condition.[9]

In the Islamic encounter with modernity, particularly via political colonization that hoisted constitutional nation-states upon Muslims and Orientalist knowledge-regimes that defined Islam as an essentially legalist religion, the place of law became much more central in life than it ever was in the classical period. As a result of this, "It is difficult not to view the appeal of the legal-supremacist conceptualization [of Islam] as stemming, in considerable part, from the fact that the authority-claim to which it subscribes is the dominant one in our own modern historical moment."[10] Even if Muslims were able to return *en masse* to being steeped in the riches of the high classical traditions of law, theology, philosophy, metaphysics, etc., would drawing upon these existing perspectives suffice in handling the *nomocentric* organization of modernity? A traditionalist may contend that precisely in

---

9. Shahab Ahmed, *What Is Islam? The Importance of Being Islamic* (Princeton, NJ: Princeton University Press, 2016), 125.
10. Ibid.

returning to the sources of Islamic intellectual history this nomocentrism would be dissolved, subverted, qualified, or in some way transformed, but to do so, one would not only need to provide an alternative political organization to the nation-state—and one which must also successfully coexist alongside nation-states; something that was not a requirement for pre-modern political entities—but also grapple with the ways that modern technologies encourage a nomocentric organization through facilitating surveillance, for example. The traditionalist could respond that one need not simply reproduce the exact forms of classical legal and political perspectives but rather—as Naeem suggests in the above-quoted passage—turn to Islam as a source of *principles* that are capable of context-specific renewal and integration of truths wherever they may originate. Here, the traditionalist's project is likely to be frustrated precisely because of their insufficient acknowledgment of the divides and tensions within traditionalism itself: there are many self-understood traditionalists who would insist on reproducing pre-modern forms of political organization and classical frameworks and approaches to law as the response to modernity, and this segment of traditionalists will oppose the "higher principles" approach of more metaphysically-minded Muslims.

Against those who present traditionalism as a dynamic middle path superior to the shared pathologies of the puritanical reformists and modernists, I propose that all three of these factions are similarly entangled in a paradigm of *repetition*. Regardless of the affiliation, there is an uncritical adoption and valorization of a particular set of methodologies or values used for critique, but not deeply exposed to the criticisms from the other factions. The Muslim process thinker Muhammad Iqbal gives voice to this dysfunction in his *Reconstruction of Religious Thought in Islam* when he proclaims, drawing inspiration from Thomas Hobbes, that "to have a succession of identical thoughts and feelings is to have no thoughts and feelings at all. Such is the lot of most Muslim countries today. They are mechanically repeating old values."[11] Likewise, Alfred North Whitehead, a major progenitor of process-relational thought, speaks poetically about this pathology of repetition towards the end of his magnum opus, *Process and Reality*, offering a vision of harmony between order and novelty: "Order is not sufficient. What is required is something much more complex. It is order entering upon novelty; so that the massiveness of order does not degenerate into mere repetition; and so that the novelty is always reflected upon the background of a system."[12]

Whitehead's thought, and the process tradition more broadly, teaches that novelty is a fundamental aspect of ontology—and this basic feature of reality is something that demands dynamic, vital responses while also being something that provides the intellectual, aesthetic, and spiritual material which can be incorporated into the process of adaptive responsiveness. As such, the repetition of classical sources from the traditionalist or the scripturalist-literalist repetition of the puritanical reformist are like dead organisms—no longer able to bring sustenance into their internal constitution, cut off from reciprocal relationship with the environment that is the basis of ecological existence. These forms of repetition foreclose the possibility of new *modes* of thinking and being, yet such novel forms may be precisely what is required by the moment. What is unique about the puritanical reformists, however, is that their literalism leads them to uncritically accept certain aspects of modernity—as can be seen in the techno-capitalist bent of a *nation-state* such as Saudi Arabia—so by lacking a more sophisticated methodology for interpretation and simply regurgitating *naqli* material they are left with few resources for grappling with developments and challenges that have no easy analogy in sacred texts.

---

11. Muhammad Iqbal, *The Reconstruction of Religious Thought in Islam* (Stanford, Calif.: Stanford University Press, 2013), 129.
12. Alfred North Whitehead, *Process and Reality*, edited by David Ray Griffin and Donald W. Sherburne (New York, NY: Free Press, 1979), 339.

The repetition of the Islamic modernist—who often repeats the forms of Western modernity in an Islamic idiom—fares no better, as they lack the deep connection with tradition that would allow for the novelty of modernity to be "reflected upon the background of a system," which is in turn what would allow for genuine discernment in deciding how to incorporate this material. Without this, the repetition of the Islamic modernist will often take the form of a skin graft that is incompatible with the unique and individual physiological patient, conditioning a harmful immune response incompatible with healing. An additional problem here is that the Western modernity that is repeated is often seen as universal, whereas this too is historically contingent and of a certain context, so the project of modernizing Islam risks introducing certain reforms which in time are shown to be mere fads of a given age, or simply no longer vital and applicable to a more contemporary context. Here again, Iqbal is incisive, emphasizing the necessity of continuity with the past and appreciation for the community-constituting value of the non-rational ritual elements of religion—

> No people can afford to reject their past entirely, for it is their past that has made their personal identity. And in a society like Islam, the problem of a revision of old institutions becomes still more delicate, and the responsibility of the reformer assumes a far more serious aspect. … even the immutability of socially harmless rules relating to eating and drinking, purity or impurity, has a life-value of its own, inasmuch as it tends to give such society a specific inwardness, and further secures that external and internal uniformity which counteracts the forces of heterogeneity always latent in a society of a composite character. The critic of these institutions must, therefore, try to secure, before he undertakes to handle them, a clear insight into the ultimate significance of the social experiment

embodied in Islam. He must look at their structure, not from the standpoint of social advantage or disadvantage to this or that country, but from the point of view of the larger purpose which is being gradually worked out in the life of mankind as a whole.[13]

A process-relational framework, as a *non-modern* philosophical system,[14] has the potential to avoid the pitfalls of these three forms of repetition while also incorporating the important insights from traditionalists, reformists, and modernists. It may also help provide fresh ontological insights to ground a developmental, contextual approach to Islamic theology, jurisprudence, ethics, and spirituality that nonetheless maintains deep contact with earlier projects in each of these veins.

---

13. Iqbal, *Reconstruction*, 132-33.
14. In *Object-Oriented Ontology: A New Theory of Everything* (Pelican Books, 2018), Graham Harman discusses the *non-modern* philosophy of French theorist Bruno Latour which features "a 'flat ontology' that erases the distinction between subject and object as an obsession of modern philosophy" (217). Harman continues "we can say the same of Alfred North Whitehead, who also steadfastly refused to see the human perception of a tree as anything radically different in kind from the wind's interaction with that tree" (Ibid.). Inspired by non-modern philosophers such as Latour and Whitehead who rejected ontological binaries between subjects and objects or the phenomenal and the noumenal that are quintessential features of modern modes of thought, process-relational thinkers find themselves in a particularly advantageous position to critique modernity *from the outside* while also providing perspectives more deeply in conversation with modern thought than is the case with even many of the more philosophically robust traditionalist critiques of modernity (see René Guénon, *Crisis of the Modern World*, and Huston Smith, *Beyond the Postmodern Mind: The Place of Meaning in a Global Civilization*). This also helps distinguish a process-relational approach to Islam from Islamic modernism, as even if some of the systematic frameworks being employed were initially developed in the contemporary West, the content and presuppositions of these frameworks are categorically different from those involved in what is typically referred to as "modern philosophy." These non-modern schemes of thought are even further removed from modern ideas than is typically the case with postmodern thought (though like "traditionalism," postmodernism is often a vague and under-differentiated signifier), as even in this later case are the modern suppositions of ontologically reified subjects and objects often preserved.

Along with the traditionalists, process-relational thinking affirms the value of a deep engagement with and appreciation for what has been handed down through tradition. However, the *form* of this appreciation is different between the two perspectives. The traditionalist typically venerates the *content* of Islamic intellectual and spiritual traditions, looking to maintain or revive particular methods, perspectives, or frameworks. The process-relational thinker sees value in this traditionalist project but is ultimately more focused on novel modes of thought that re-enact the powerful *movements* witnessed in Islamic history rather than merely retrieving its content. How can we, as contemporary Muslims, encourage similar movements toward justice as the Prophet (ﷺ) did in his own time? How can we, like the early Islamic theologians who drew upon Greek philosophy and science, take the best philosophical and scientific material in our own day and use these to clarify theological issues? How can we, like the Ashʿarites, Abū Ḥāmid al-Ghazālī, or Ibn Taymiyyah, chart the proper bounds of instrumental reason and critique the excesses of heavy-handed rationalism—something especially urgent in our times when the appropriation of scientific rationalism by global capitalism is a significant source for the cataclysmic degradation of the natural world. Of course, we may—and ought to—draw direct inspiration from the ideas of any of the above-mentioned figures, but we need not confine our thought to only the frameworks which have been handed down—certainly, that is not what these great figures of Islamic history themselves were doing. On the contrary, all such figures were involved in essentially creative acts of thinking, seeking to appropriate, modify, synthesize, and expand upon received ideas in dynamic ways so as to produce something more holistic, comprehensive, and apt for the unique issues of their own times.

In the unwillingness of traditionalists to sign off on this type of creative work, one discovers a strange "metaphysics of modernity," which, although not often stated explicitly, seems to suggest that there is something fundamental that has shifted in the advent of modernity—a genuinely *ontological* shift—where the proper intellectual disposition in a religious context may now only look towards the past and its philosophical and theological artifacts, rather than towards novelty, towards new horizons of thought.[15] Just as Muhammad (ﷺ) is known to be the "Seal of the Prophets," it seems that many traditionalists (and puritanical reformists) have smuggled a notion of a "Seal of Creative Thought" into Islamic dogma. There is no specific individual who is clearly identified as this "Seal"—though it does make one think of the superfluous claims that "al-Ghazālī foreclosed philosophy in the Islamic world"—but there is nonetheless a palpable sense that genuinely creative philosophy and theology is something only of the past, no longer alive or permissible in our times. This perspective is particularly odd, as it is not something that is justified on any genuinely traditional source—either the puritanical reformists are right in their *naqli* protests that independent philosophy and theology are essentially anti-Islamic and thus whole swaths of pivotal Muslim thinkers must be discounted more or less wholesale, or the doors of creative

---

15. Those who identify with the Traditionalist school are more explicit in these ideas, hence Seyyed Hossein Nasr in *Knowledge and the Sacred* (New York: State University of New York Press, 1989): "One could say that the traditional worlds were essentially good and accidentally evil, and the modern world essentially evil and accidentally good. Tradition is therefore opposed in principle to modernism" (76) What is odd about this perspective, however, is that it seems to suggest some metaphysical principle or force at work in modernity which is uniquely able to subvert the *theophanic* relationship of God towards creation—which these such Traditionalists typically presume—which was not at play during any other point in sacred history. Nasr tries to qualify this polemic against such criticisms with points such as "complete falsehood or evil could not exist since every mode of existence implies some element of that truth and goodness which in their purity belong to the Source of all existence" (Ibid.) but this falls flat in light of much Traditionalist rhetoric which engages in equivocation between *modernism*—i.e. the ideological underpinnings behind the values and modes of thought that emerged in Europe sometime in the mid- to late-second millennium and which spread globally in the coming centuries—and anything that is not explicitly "traditional" which nonetheless exists in the contemporary period. Hence the importance of the point expanded in note 14 that process-relational thought is, though *contemporary*, ultimately *non-modern*.

thought remain open just as they did during the classical period. Of course, there are ways to justify this type of perspective, which ironically requires creative, independent thought or drawing on sources not contained in the classical tradition, as is the method of the modernist. So, this is an essentially paradoxical or self-undermining scheme.

Contrary to this implicit notion of the "Seal of Creative Thought," the process-relational Muslim thinker may say with Fazlur Rahman and many Muslim modernists "that the process of questioning and changing a tradition—in the interests of preserving or restoring its normative quality in the case of its normative elements—can continue indefinitely and that there is no fixed or privileged point at which the predetermining effective history is immune from such questioning."[16] Where Muslim modernists typically failed, however, was in turning this same mode of critical thought in the direction of the intellectual foundations of modernism itself. Though not always entirely uncritical in orientation, one finds a significant and eager adoption amongst early Muslim modernists, particularly of those aspects of modernism which now so clearly bear great responsibility for the crises of our era: metanarratives of progress and the rationalist-materialist supremacy of scientism.[17] Here, critiques of modernism found within process-relational philosophy may prove especially helpful for Muslim

---

16. Fazlur Rahman, *Islam and Modernity: Transformation of an Intellectual Tradition* (Chicago, IL: University of Chicago Press, 1984), 11.

17. In his article "Religion Versus Science," quoted in *Contemporary Debates in Islam: An Anthology of Modernist and Fundamentalist Thought*, edited by Mansoor Moaddel and Kamran Talattof (New York, NY: St. Martin's Press, 2000), the inimitable modernist thinker Sayyid Jamāl al-Dīn al-Afghānī sets science and religion in opposition, stating "the Muslim religion has tried to stifle science and stop its progress" (25) and talks of the necessity to overcome the essential, anti-intellectual dogmatism of religion in order to "achieve the same degree of civilization [as the West]" (Ibid.). Reading such statements with contemporary eyes, there is a genuine *naïveté* palpable in al-Afghānī's uncritical internalization of modern metanarratives of progress and colonialist notions of more or less developed cultures and civilizations. Lumbard's polemics against Muslim modernists puts the situation in stark relief when he suggests that these thinkers "were so awed by the technological achievements of Western civilization that they freely surrendered the ground of intellectuality to the secular

intellectuals seeking to tread a middle path between an uncritical buy-in of perspectives and values from Western modernity on the one hand and a cloistered and narrow traditionalism on the other.

Turning now to the puritanical reformists, even here, there is something of value that is affirmed by a process-relational perspective: namely, that returning directly to sacred sources, without the mediation of potentially ossified institutionalized religious authorities, opens up the possibility for renewal in the now. Such material may serve as a fount for fresh inspiration in all contexts. However, against the heavy-handed literalism of this camp, the process-relational thinker insists—here, drawing upon Whitehead's ontology of becoming—that the attentive reading of scripture is never an act that occurs in a vacuum: there are always *prehensions* outside of the text itself which are entering in upon the process of understanding, whether these be influences such as socio-cultural conditioning, received intellectual ideas, or more personally-grounded influences such as one's own emotional state at the time of reading, narratives from one's own life, or one's particular psychological disposition. It is neither possible nor desirable to "purify" an interpretation of revelation or the Sunnah of these relations—interconnection is an ontological fact. However, those working with these sources are still doomed to a decadent subjectivism or relativism of interpretation. Precisely because process-relational thinking is *non-modern*, it rejects the binary between subject and object presumed in this anxiety. The process of engaging sacred sources as a wellspring of inspiration is essentially *transjective*—inseparable from the objective web of relations that co-constitute both the reader and the text while also involving inherent subjective creativity in how these relations are taken up and transmuted into a particular *subjective* form. In light of the ontological principles of interconnectivity

---

humanistic and scientistic (as opposed to scientific) world-view that gave rise to them" (*Islam, Fundamentalism, and the Betrayal of Tradition*, 40).

and becoming, all encounters with the Qur'an or the Sunnah of the Prophet (ﷺ) have an aspect of irreducible novelty. This can either be creatively appropriated or struggled against in vain.

While the literalist-textualist hermeneutics of the puritanical reformists take the latter approach and treat this as something which must be overcome, the process-relational interpreter sees these dynamics of novelty as an opening. Helpful in clarifying this situation is Michael Muhammad Knight, who draws upon the rhizomatic process thought of Gilles Deleuze to suggest that—

> The Qur'an as a rhizome is both the Qur'an as a body of text between two covers and the infinite modes by which the Qur'an can connect with the circulating intensities of the world. When the effects of the Qur'an change through these encounters, it's not a matter of 'influence,' 'imitation,' 'borrowing,' or 'syncretism,' because there is no possibility of a Qur'an existing before the encounter; the Qur'an *is* the Qur'an's rhizome with the world.[18]

Knight's Deleuzian insights into Qur'anic exegesis treat the scripture as always open to *deterritorializations* which reveal novel *lines of flight,* leading to new possibilities for a sense of connection with the Divine, solidarity in religious communities, and realization of greater agency and responsibility for ethical action in the cosmos—among many other prototypical religious values. In a move exemplary of the balance and of a process-relational approach to reading sacred sources, Knight claims that—

---

18. Michael Muhammad Knight, *Sufi Deleuze: Secretions of Islamic Atheism* (New York: Fordham University Press, 2023), 54.

The rhizomatic Qur'an plugs into both exotericisms and esotericisms, though it is not always a given that one enables movement that the other restrains. At first glance, it would appear that the batin is always the key to deterritorialization and the zahir always reterrirtorializes; but in a batini regime, a zahiri cutting edge of scripturalist fundamentalism would offer deterrirotializing escapes from the master's strata.[19]

Likewise, a process-relational framework for engaging the interface between Islam and modernity identifies the dynamic of repetition (territorialization in Knight's Deleuzian terminology) as a lurking pathology in the existing responses from modernists, traditionalists, and puritanical reformists. However, grounded in a dynamic and relational vision of ontology, process-relational thinkers may also find resources for creative responses to the conditions of modernity within each of these camps. What is important is not the *content* but the *context*—does the deployment of these ideas, being as they are in critical relation to Islamic intellectual traditions, the discoveries, power, and institutions of modernity, and sacred sources in Islam, allow for a productive balance of order and novelty? Or do these ideas lead to a foreclosing of creative and vital thought, falling back upon a mere repetition that denies the ontological reality of novelty?

By grounding Islamic responses to modernity in a process-relational framework, contemporary Muslim thinkers may avoid the uncritical repetitions of the modernists, traditionalists, and puritanical reformists while also placing many of the inspiring and creative projects happening in current Islamic discourse in a broader context. From ideas on *maqāṣid al-sharī'a* to Fazlur Rahman's axiological hermeneutical approach to the Qur'an, process-relational thinking has the

---

19. Ibid., 57.

potential to incorporate the insights of such projects into a cohesive framework, allowing for a more holistic and dynamic response to modernity that is through and through *Islamic* without being restrained to the creativity of the past.

Bibliography

- Ahmed, Shahab. *What Is Islam? The Importance of Being Islamic.* Princeton, NJ: Princeton University Press, 2016.
- Harman, Graham. *Object Oriented Ontology: A New Theory of Everything.* Pelican Books, 2018.
- Iqbal, Muhammad. *The Reconstruction of Religious Thought in Islam.* Stanford, Calif.: Stanford University Press, 2013.
- Knight, Michael Muhammad. *Sufi Deleuze: Secretions of Islamic Atheism.* New York: Fordham University Press, 2023.
- Lumbard, Joseph E. B, editor. *Islam, Fundamentalism, and the Betrayal of Tradition: Essays by Western Muslim Scholars.* Revised and Expanded Edition. Bloomington, Ind.: World Wisdom, 2009.
- Moaddel, Mansoor and Kamran Talattof. *Contemporary Debates in Islam: An Anthology of Modernist and Fundamentalist Thought.* New York, NY: St. Martin's Press, 2000
- Qutb, Sayyid. Milestones. New Delhi: Abdus Sami, 2002.
- Rahman, Fazlur. *Islam and Modernity: Transformation of an Intellectual Tradition.* Chicago, IL: University of Chicago Press, 1984.
- Nasr, Seyyed Hossein. *Knowledge and the Sacred.* New York: State University of New York Press, 1989.
- Whitehead, Alfred North. *Process and Reality.* Edited by David Ray Griffin and Donald W. Sherburne. New York, NY: Free Press, 1979.

TEN HOPEFUL IDEAS:
In Conversation with Jared Morningstar

JAY MCDANIEL, Willis Holmes Professor of Religious Studies at Hendrix College in Arkansas, and founder of www.openhorizons.org which focuses on exploring a process outlook on life and way of living in the world.

In *Process Relational Thought and Islam: Proposing a Novel Framework for Constructive Engagement with Modernity*, Jared Morningstar offers a cautious but hopeful essay. He proposes that:

- novelty is part of the very make-up of the universe.
- three forms of Islamic thought—modernism, traditionalism, and puritanical reformism—are trapped in repetition, albeit in different ways.
- with help from a process-relational approach to life, they can grow beyond the trap, recognize a continuity between novelty and tradition, and work together to help create a new and better world for Muslims and all.

This new and better world will not be pre-modern or post-modern but rather, as it were, metamodern. It will build upon values from the past even as it ventures forth in new directions.

I find Morningstar's openness to each of the three traditions interesting and inspiring. I hope he is right. Of course, the future is open, and there are many circumstances in the world today that point toward a less hopeful future: global climate change, widening economic gaps, authoritarianism, war and the threat of nuclear war, and the deadening effects of patriarchy. For process-relational thinkers, as for everyone else, hope for what John Sanders might call a more "nurturant" future is fragile indeed. Emily Dickinson had it right, "Hope is a thing with feathers," and a small bird at that.

In my response, I build upon Morningstar's note of hope by offering ten more ideas from the process tradition that might help Muslims, Christians, and Jews work toward a better world together. I am the Chair of the Board of Directors of the Cobb Institute for Process and Practice, founded by John Cobb. I am also on the leadership team for a multi-faith organization called Process and Faith. And I work closely with a local mosque where I live, helping them facilitate interfaith offerings. These experiences, along with a lifelong study of process theology, inform my thinking.

Please note: each of the ten ideas, and all of them together, can be derived from sources internal to the Islamic[12], Christian[3], and Jewish[4] traditions; all are "open and relational" in spirit; and while the philosopher Whitehead can indeed by an ally, appeals to Whitehead are not necessary. Today many process theologians are less "Whiteheadian" than they used to be. They think in a Whiteheadian mode, but they do not want to fit all things into a Whiteheadian box. I am among them.

---

1. https://www.openhorizons.org/three-paradigms-for-an-emerging-islamic-process-theology.html
2. https://www.openhorizons.org/three-paradigms-for-an-emerging-islamic-process-theology.html
3. https://cobb.institute/educators-toolbox/christian-process-theology-marjorie-suchocki/
4. https://cobb.institute/educators-toolbox/jewish-process-theology/

Social Ideals

Our conference is on the social and political implications of an open and relational approach to life; I begin with a word about the social aspirations of the process movement today. We in the process community (Muslims, Jews, Christians, Hindus, and others) encourage four aspirational ideals, four hopes[5], which, in our view, can be embodied by people of many faiths and no faith. You can find these hopes named on the Process and Faith[6] website and further articulated in slideshows offered by the Cobb Institute. The four aspirational ideals are:

1. Individual well-being: the hope that individual human beings can enjoy significant degrees of wholeness that includes material and spiritual dimensions of their lives. See Spirituality in Process Perspective.[7] See also Beauty in Process Perspective[8].
2. Just and compassionate communities: the hope that humans can build communities that are creative, compassionate, participatory, humane to animals, and good for the earth, with no one left behind.
3. Planetary well-being: the hope that the planet as a whole can flourish with multiple forms of life, with people living with respect and care for life. See Ecological Civilization and Just and Compassionate Community.[9]
4. Holistic Thinking: the hope that human beings can develop forms of holistic or organic thinking—drawing from philosophy, science, theology, and art—that lend themselves to respect

---

[5]. https://cobb.institute/educators-toolbox/four-hopes-of-the-process-movement/
[6]. https://processandfaith.org/
[7]. https://cobb.institute/educators-toolbox/process-spirituality/
[8]. https://cobb.institute/educators-toolbox/beauty-process-theology/
[9]. https://cobb.institute/educators-toolbox/ecological-civilization-and-just-compassionate-communities/

and care for life. For a process version of such a worldview, see *A Process Worldview,*[10] and *Fourteen Process Transformations.*[11]

A Process Worldview

Typically, when process theologians and philosophers speak of a process worldview, they have at least five ideas in mind:[12]

1. Inter-becoming: Everything is connected; all beings inter-become. There are no isolated substances. The universe is in process.
2. Intrinsic Value: All living beings have value for themselves and for others. All living beings have intrinsic value as well as instrumental value.
3. Purposive Universe: The universe is purposive: beauty, creativity, and life are part of its very makeup.
4. Creativity: The universe is creative; the idea of entirely dead matter is an illusion. Novelty is part of existence.
5. The Earth Community: humans are part of, not apart from, this larger whole and find fulfillment in living with respect and care for all life, human and non-human.

Divine Nurturing

To the ideas just named, many process theologians will, of course, add one more: the idea of what John Sanders would call a "nurturant God" and Thomas Oord[13] would call an "open and relational" God. Some will consider this the most important idea. The open and relational movement in many settings is known primarily for its view of God and secondarily for its view of the universe.

---

10. https://cobb.institute/educators-toolbox/a-process-worldview-jay-mcdaniel/
11. https://cobb.institute/educators-toolbox/14-process-transformations/
12. https://cobb.institute/educators-toolbox/a-process-worldview-lynn-de-jonghe/
13. https://cobb.institute/educators-toolbox/open-relational-theology/

In process theology, a nurturant God is "nurturant" in two ways:

1. actively, as a continuous influence in the world through the provision of ideals and fresh possibilities to live by.
2. receptively, as an empathic companion to the world's joys and sufferings. In both respects, God is in process: that is, affecting and affected by what happens in the world. God is relational.

This does not mean that God is *only* in process. Some process theologians, and I am among them, also speak of a timeless side of God: that is, an aspect of God that is beyond time and space. Whitehead called it the primordial nature of God, seeing it as the side of God that is aware of pure potentialities (eternal object) even before they are actualized in and by the world. For my part, I see a recognition of a timeless side of God as important to Islamic theology and many traditional Christians. As I see things, the good news is that you can be part of the process movement without subscribing to a process understanding of God. Nine of ten ideas are fine.

I must also note that there are non-theistic process theologians who accept all nine ideas above but not the tenth. Some are in the West and some in China, where Daoist influences make more sense to them than Abrahamic approaches.

When it comes to hopes for a better world, we, in the process and faith community, welcome everyone who identifies with the aspirations and worldview for one reason or another. Yes, with Morningstar, we think that there is something like novelty within the depths of things. And, with Morningstar, the very Soul of the universe, however named, is a lure to think in fresh ways. But we know that people need not be process theologians to add goodness and beauty to a world in need. Goodness and beauty are the most important.

OPEN AND RELATIONAL THEOLOGY AND ITS SOCIAL AND POLITICAL IMPLICATIONS:
Perspectives from Progressive Islam

ADIS DUDERIJA, Senior Lecturer in Study of Islam and Society, Griffith University, Co-founder Network of Spiritual Progressives Australia, Executive Committee Member Religions for Peace Australia. For more information, see https://experts.griffith.edu.au/7439-adis-duderija.

Let me start with outlining my basic premises. Our worldview shapes how we conceptualize the Divine (and vice versa). How we conceptualize the Divine, in turn, shapes our ethical-moral compass and our values. Our ethical-moral compass and values shape our attitudes and views on how social and political life should be organized.

Not unlike other major world religious traditions and Christianity in particular, the Islamic worldview is based on the idea of a partnership between the Divine as the source of awe-inspiring Majesty, Beauty, and Goodness and humanity, which has been tasked with a special ethical responsibility to embody and enact these God like values and attributes at both the level of individuals and societies seeking to create conditions that contribute to flourishing and well-being of all of God's creation.

My other point of self-positioning is that I have been, for nearly two decades now, a theoretician and vocal proponent of progressive Muslim thought /progressive Islam. The most significant delineating features of this approach to the Islamic tradition can be summarized as follows:

1. A subscription to a panentheistic concept of the Divine and a form of Islamic open-relational/process theology
2. Emphasis on creative, critical, and innovative thought based on epistemological openness and methodological fluidity,
3. Rationalist and contextualist approaches to Islamic theology and ethics,
4. Political governance based on principles of constitutional democracy
5. Islamic liberation theology,
6. Affirmation of conceptual compatibility of the Islamic normative tradition with modern human rights era declarations such as the UDHR.
7. Affirmation of religious pluralism (Duderija 2011; Duderija 2017)

As I have argued elsewhere (Duderija 2017) these major characteristics of what constitutes a progressive Islamic worldview also constitute its most important normative imperatives. The concept of the normative imperative for the proponents of progressive Muslim thought refers to certain theological, moral, and ethical principles that ought to guide the principled actions of those who believe in the Islamic message, and which are considered to be in accordance with the foundational Islamic textual sources.

Importantly, however, these normative imperatives are considered applicable to all humanity since they are premised on the belief in pre-theoretical and pre-conventional concepts of truth and justice that do not presuppose faith. In the context of Islam as a religious tradition, this translates itself into the idea of Islam being an ethical-religious worldview whose anchoring value is the idea of 'ethics of responsibility' in which humans, as God's partners, have the responsibility to act justly and fight for justice even if it is against their own self-interest.

This idea is conveyed eloquently by one of the leading progressive Muslim thinkers, Khaled Abou El Fadl (2014, 116–117), who states that "[t]he religious conscience should be invoked in all situations that could create a greater sanctity and understanding of the sacred nature of human life". In other words, the normative imperative is an affirmative obligation of the idea that "the religious conscience must be thoroughly engaged with everything that elevates human beings from ugliness to goodness" (Sachedina, 2008, 89). Sachedina (2008), another leading progressive Muslim scholar, uses the terminology of 'ethical necessity', which more or less corresponds to what is termed a 'normative imperative' in this study. For Sachedina, ethical necessity is "an action that is rationally required (wujub 'aqlı) because it is based on moral norms that follow from human nature which not only serve as the underlying framework for natural law but also Islamic natural law" (Sachedina, 2008, p. 89) if approached from the standpoint of rational theological ethics to which progressive Muslim thought subscribes.

In philosophical terms, the idea of the normative imperative is premised on the presupposition that, contrary to much of the Western contemporary liberal ethical-political theory, it is possible to make a philosophically coherent argument that human beings have real moral duties (MacDonald, 2012). As a result, it is possible to deliberate and ultimately form a judgment about the truth of different moral and ethical claims on the basis of one's commitment to ethics of responsibility and humility, and hence the legitimacy of diversity.

However, this deliberation process about truth and justice is dialogical and considers the diversity of perspectives integral to it. Hence, the above-described concept of the normative imperative is not tantamount to the belief in crude moral absolutism and accompanying fundamentalist and totalitarian approaches to truth, the politics of truth, and its socio-political ramifications.

This is because progressive Muslim thought gives due consideration to the idea that these moral and ethical ways of acting manifest take different forms and shapes in different socio-cultural and historical contexts and that they are, in principle, subject to evolution and ever better but never fully exhaustible approximations of Divine attributes of Majesty (jalal) and Beauty(jamal).

Unfortunately, with very few notable exceptions, the conceptualization of jalal and jamal in the Islamic intellectual tradition has endorsed a concept of the divine that sanctions patriarchy and political tyranny. Moreover, mainstream Islamic theology is based on a classical theistic conceptualization of God and, therefore, suffers from the same shortcomings that process-relational philosophy and theology has rightly levelled at classical Christian theistic tradition as found in the works of scholars such as Charles Hartshorne, John Cobb Jr, David Ray Griffin, Jay McDaniel, Daniel Dombrowski, and Thomas Jay Oord.

As evident from the nature of these delineating features of progressive Islam, for the proponents of progressive Muslim thought, there is an organic and symbiotic link between the political and the hermeneutic. This has given rise to the notion of what can be termed 'social hermeneutics', which can be described as a highly participatory political endeavor enabling progressive Muslim scholar-activists to seek socio-political change within a faith-based framework.

For these actors, engaging in social hermeneutics implies that religious knowledge can act as a basis for social transformation, revolution, and collective political activism. Progressive Muslim social hermeneutics, as it is, in part, is also employed to argue for the emergence of religiously persuasive discourse on issues such as gender justice/equality, human rights, freedom of religion and democracy, the establishment of a vibrant public sphere, and increased transparency and accountability of political structures and institutions, especially in Muslim-majority contexts.

Importantly unlike the vast majority of conservative forms of political Islam, progressive Islam is cosmopolitan in outlook and embraces constitutional democracy and contemporary ideas on human rights, gender equality, and vibrant civil society.

It is noteworthy that many proponents of progressive Muslim thought are women. They, in particular, are dislodging the epistemic privilege enjoyed by traditionally educated, exclusively male religious scholars and clergy. In this context, they play a major role in shifting the locus of authority and normativity in Islamic discourses.

With the focus on gender equality, and particularly the reform of traditional jurisprudence (fiqh) pertaining to Muslim family law being one of the pillars of both their scholarship and their activism, progressive Muslim scholars subscribe to the idea, stemming from feminist discourses, that the personal is political, thus bringing issues of gender and the Muslim juristic tradition in general to the forefront of Muslim politics.

Progressive Islam as form of Islamic liberation theology:

As noted above, progressive Islam is a form of Islamic liberation theology. The proponents of progressive Muslim thought argue that developing an Islamic liberation theology is crucial for Muslims in the 21st century. They cite several reasons for this necessity:

1. Traumatic legacy of colonialism: Progressive Muslims believe that the historical experience of colonialism has had a lasting impact on Muslim societies, leading to social, economic, and political injustices that need to be addressed through a liberation theology approach.
2. Growing wealth disparity: There is a widening gap between the rich and the poor, both in general and within the Muslim community. Progressive Muslims argue that an Islamic liberation theology can help address this inequality and promote economic justice.

3. Rise of Islamic puritanism/fundamentalism: The spread of puritanical and fundamentalist interpretations of Islam, often in alliance with neo-liberal capitalism, is seen as a challenge to progressive Muslim thought. They believe that an Islamic liberation theology can counter these conservative ideologies and promote a more inclusive and socially just understanding of Islam.
4. Political, economic, and social impotence of mainstream political Islam: Progressive Muslims criticize mainstream political Islam for its inability to bring about meaningful change and address social injustices. They argue that a liberation theology approach is needed to challenge the status quo and advocate for the rights of marginalized and underprivileged groups.

Abdenur Prado, a vocal supporter of Islamic liberation theology, highlights the obstacles posed by non-progressive currents in Islam. He argues that these currents, with their emphasis on extreme morality and puritanism, prevent critical thinking and hinder the analysis of the root causes of social injustices (Prado,n.d)

Similarly, Samir Amin criticizes non-progressive political Islam for its reactionary stance and its co-optation by capitalism and imperialism. He argues that such forms of political Islam are incompatible with the ideals and objectives of Islamic liberation theology, as they are not anti-imperialist but merely anti-western or anti-Christian (Amin 2007).

For proponents of progressive Muslim thought, the revival of Islamic liberation theology requires a radical reform of traditional understandings of Islamic law (Shari'a). This includes rethinking concepts, aims, and objectives of Islamic theology, ethics, and law, transforming Islamic finance and economics for economic justice, and aligning Islamic politics with the values and objectives of liberation theology.

A stelar exemplifier of Islamic liberation theology is the late Hassan Hanafi (d.2021), a former Professor of Philosophy at Cairo University. Hasan Hanafi is a prominent Islamic liberation theology scholar who has contributed significantly to various fields. Hanafi's scholarship involves reconstructing Islamic heritage through a new historicist and critical interpretation, reassessing Western culture through a critical approach, and building a new hermeneutic of religious culture on a global scale that promotes liberation and positive action for all. One of Hanafi's main projects is al-Turath wal Tajdid, (Heritage and Revival) which involves reviving the tradition (Turath) in the light of modern imperatives. This project aims to reconnect with the hidden Turath values consistent with liberation theology's ideals and objectives (Duderija 2017, 91-94).

Hanafi's Islamic liberation theology takes the form of what he calls the Islamic left (al-Yasar al-Islami), which seeks to promote a comprehensive renaissance of Islamic civilization through projects such as *al-Turath wa al-Tajdid*. The Islamic Left is grounded in the Turath and is not a rejection of it. It is part of an international movement of liberation and deals with issues such as the relationship between religion and revolution, Islamic unity, social justice, and freedom of speech.

Hanafi's Islamic Left is critical of imperialism, Zionism, and capitalism, which affect the Muslim-majority world, leading to poverty, oppression, and underdevelopment. The Islamic Left emphasizes socioeconomic justice and demands wealth distribution to bridge the gap between the rich and the poor (Duderija 2017, 91-94).

Hanafi's Islamic Left has strong affinities with Christian liberation theology, and he seeks to develop an Islamic equivalent. Hanafi believes that the main function of theology is to act as a springboard for garnering support to end all kinds of oppression and exploitation. He argues that an internal re-examination of inherited Muslim belief systems is necessary because these often mirror existing general power structures within Muslim societies, which are elitist in nature.

Hanafi proposes that the interests of the masses need to be defended by educating them in the belief systems of opposition. He believes this pedagogical function of political theology is necessary in the context of the contemporary Muslim world because the ruling state powers are employing what he terms an "Absolutist Theology" to maintain the unjust status quo. Hanafi finds inspiration in Mu'tazilite public opposition to power and their justice-based theory of Unity as a kind of pre-modern form of Islamic liberation theology that he wants to revive among contemporary Muslims.

To achieve this goal, Hanafi takes the view that it is imperative to reformulate and reinterpret the major concepts in Islamic theology such as including the idea of God's Oneness(Tawhid), Wahy (revelation), 'Aqida (doctrine) and the so-called five pillars of Islam (Duderija 2017, 91-94).Overall, for reasons outlined above progressive Muslim thought sees Islamic liberation theology as an imperative for addressing social injustices, promoting economic justice, and challenging conservative ideologies within the Muslim community.

Conclusion:

As discussed above, progressive Muslim thought as a form of Islamic process theology, with its panentheistic concept of the Divine, has wide-ranging socio-political implications, not only in Muslim majority contexts but also globally. Its worldview is premised on the imperative of adopting a creative and critical approach to knowledge by means of epistemological and methodological openness; the possibility of epistemological, moral, and ethical progress; the imperative of gender justice and non-patriarchal interpretations of Islam as examples of rediscovering the ethical in Islamic law; the utmost concern for the rights of all, especially those on the margins and the vulnerable, non-monopolization of religious truth and a contextualist approach to the normative fountainheads grounded in a concept of an open-relational God rooted in justice, goodness, mercy, and beauty. Progressive Muslims firmly believe that the Islamic tradition (turath), if approached and conceptualized in harmony with these imperatives, has the necessary intellectual resources to turn them into a tangible and concrete reality.

Furthermore, as explained above, progressive Muslim scholars, such as in the case of Hassan Hanafi, have moved away from mainstream accommodationist interpretations of Islamic theology because they are seen as incompatible with the ideals, values, and objectives of Islamic liberation theology. They have engaged in systematic and creative efforts to reinterpret fundamental concepts of their creed, such as Tawhid (Oneness of God), jihad (struggle), Wahy (revelation), and Mu'min (believer), using sophisticated methodologies and hermeneutics to conceptualize them as anthropomorphic liberatory concepts rather than purely theological ones.

Progressive Muslim scholars, as liberation theologians, engage in a "multiple critique" of forces and structures responsible for perpetuating oppression and injustice, regardless of whether they come from outside the Turath or within and regardless of the faith, race, or gender-based identities of their victims. They relentlessly scrutinize these forces and structures to promote liberation and social justice.

All of the imperatives of progressive Islam, as identified above, are premised on the idea of a uniquely Muslim contribution to broader universal discourses on many pressing socio-political and ethical conundrums facing humanity today. As such, integrating these imperatives self-consciously into the Islamic tradition will, hopefully, lead to the recognition of the Islamic tradition as an important and constructive contributor to these very discourses.

In the final analysis, it is imperative for us to recognize that our concept of God has important implications—not only for what kind of abstract theological beliefs we might hold but also what kind of ethical values we should abide by. And these ethical values form the backbone of the societal and political norms and ideals we consider normative for human life.

Bibliography

- Amin.S. *Political Islam in the Service of Imperialism*, http://monthlyreview.org/2007/12/01/political-islam-in-the-service-of-imperialism/, 2007.
- Duderija, A. *Constructing Religiously Ideal "Believer" and "Woman" in Islam: Neo-Traditional Salafi and Progressive Muslims' Methods of Interpretation*. United States: Palgrave Macmillan, 2011.
- Duderija, A. *The Imperatives of Progressive Islam*. United Kingdom: Routledge, 2017.
- Abou El Fadl, Khaled. *Reasoning with God: Reclaiming Shari'a in the Modern Age*. New York: Rowmann and Littlefield, 2014.
- Macdonald, Matthew A.. *Truth, Politics and Diversity: A Muslim Response to Modern Liberalism*. Carleton University, 2012.
- Prado, Abdenor. *The Need for an Islamic Liberation Theology*, http://www.dialogoglobal.com/granada/documents/Prado-The-need-for-an-Islamic-liberationtheology.pdf
- Sachedina, Abdulaziz. Islam and Challenge of Human Rights. New York: Oxford University, 2008.

THE RESPONSIBILITY OF EMBODYING GODLIKE ATTRIBUTES:
In Conversation wth Adis Duderija

DAVE ANDREWS, Director Community Praxis Cooperative, for more information, see http://www.daveandrews.com.au/.

I am thankful for the opportunity to respond to Dr Adis Duderija's paper exploring *Open And Relational Theology and its Social and Political Implications From The Perspective Of Progressive Islam*. Adis is a Muslim, and I am a Christian. Over the last five years, we have been on a journey together of mutually encouraging intra-faith and inter-faith critical engagement. Our most recent collaboration has been to co-author a provocative academic paper entitled, *Nonviolent Interfaith Solidarity Jihad - With Two Autobiographical Accounts*.

Adis is a first-generation Australian Muslim. Faced with "ethnic cleansing" unleashed in the former Yugoslavia, Adis and his family fled Bosnia and found safety as Australian refugees. He is a Lecturer in the Study of Islam and Society at Griffith University, a member of the Network of Australian Spiritual Progressives, and a world-renowned advocate of 'Progressive Islam'. Adis is totally opposed to what he calls 'Islamism.' Instead, Adis advocates a progressive, open, critical, and creative ijtihadi approach to Islam committed to liberation theology, religious pluralism, civil society, social justice, gender equality, and human rights.[1]

---

1. A. Duderija & H. Rane (2018) 'Islam And Muslims In The West – Major Issues And Debates' Palgrave Macmillan, London. p38

Adis says, "Our concept of God has important implications (for) what kind of ethical values ... form the kind of societal and political ... ideals we consider normative for human life." Over the last five years, Adis has begun to study the concept of God in process theology. He has discovered synergies between process theology and what he calls an "Intellectual Form of Sufism' in Islam." (Duderija 2011). His own ensuing Islamic open and relational understanding of God has come to underpin, support, shape, and reshape his approach to progressive Islam.

Adis still affirms the same features of Progressive Islam he has delineated in his publications over the last ten years (Duderija 2011; Duderija 2017) such as:

- 'an emphasis on epistemological openness and methodological fluidity',
- 'rationalist and contextualist approaches to Islamic theology and ethics,'
- 'political governance based on principles of constitutional democracy'
- 'Islamic liberation theology',
- 'modern human rights'
- 'religious pluralism'

However, Adis now considers an open and relational understanding of God so important that he refers to it in this presentation as Progressive Islam's primary "delineating feature." He now says the number one characteristic of Progressive Islam is "subscription" to a "panentheistic concept of the divine—an 'Islamic open-relational/process theology."(Duderija 2023)

As a matter of justice, Adis has always concentrated on critical gender issues in Islam. He frequently refers to progressive female Muslim scholars and progressive feminist Muslim discourses. He writes extensively and intensively about Islamic feminist scriptural hermeneutics and its contribution to a broader acceptance of the very concept of Islamic feminism, especially among those in Islam who might be prejudiced against feminism.

I think that the open and relational understanding of God, which Adis has developed from a progressive Muslim perspective, has been profoundly influenced by the progressive Muslim thought of many women he specifically mentions in his presentation. Let me illustrate what I mean by mentioning just one of the many progressive Muslim women scholars whose scholarship Adis engages with.

Adis cites Amina Wadud, an African-American convert to Islam, who describes herself as a "pro-faith, pro-feminist Muslim woman." Adis says Amina "constructs her non-patriarchal interpretations of the Islamic tradition on the basis of the ... Qur'anic concept of tawhid (Divine Oneness)." Tawhid for Amina "is the operating principle of equilibrium and cosmic harmony.... [T]awhid relates to relationships and developments within the social and political realms, emphasizing the unity of all human creatures beneath one Creator."

She forms the view that if human beings are truly created to be God's trustees (khilafa) on earth (Q 2:3027), then the purpose of this human agency is to work in harmony with God's purposes of justice and equity. "Being khalifah is equivalent to fulfilling one's human destiny as a moral agent, whose responsibility is to participate in upholding the harmony of the universe." She concludes, 'Women and men must occupy a relationship of horizontal reciprocity, maintaining the highest place for God in His/Her/Its uniqueness.' (Wadud 2008, 437)

Note Amina's gender-inclusive reference to God—not merely in 'Its', but in 'His' and in 'Her' uniqueness. Here is a "pro-faith, pro-feminist Muslim woman" talking about the feminine in the very nature of God. Adis and I have discussed the feminine nature of God manifest in the Bismillah many times and often discussed its open and relational, social, and political implications for our world.

The *Basmala* or *Bismillah* stands for the Arabic phrase *Bismillah ir-Rahman ir-Rahim,* a beautiful poetic phrase many Muslim friends say contains the true essence of the *Qur'an,* indeed the true essence of all religions. Every chapter of the Qur'an (except one) begins with this phrase, most commonly translated, "In the name of God, most Gracious, most Compassionate."[2]

"Bismillah" or *"bismi Allah"* means "in the name of *Allah."* "*Allah"* is not the Muslim name for God, still less the name of a Muslim God, but the Arabic name of the One True God. The Semitic roots of the word 'Allah' extend back thousands of years to the Canaanite *"Elat,"* Hebrew *"El"* and *"Elohim,"* and Aramaic *"Alaha."* To recite the Bismillah is to recall there are not many gods but One God and that One God is not Muslim, Jewish, or Christian but the One to whom we belong and who belongs to us all.[3]

In *Crossing the Threshold of Hope,* Pope John Paul II wrote, the God of the Qur'an is "ultimately a God outside of the world, a God who is only Majesty, never Emmanuel, God-with-us.' But both the *rahman* and the *rahim* enunciated in *Bismillah ir-Rahman ir-Rahim,* are derived from the Semitic root *rhm,* which "indicates something of the utmost tenderness and kindness which provides protection and nourishment" from which the creation is brought into being. The root *rhm* connotes the womb, its nourishing-tenderness, its loving-kindness. Some Muslim theologians, therefore, have referred to 'the whole of nature—that is, the universe in its entirety—as the divine womb'.[4] Thus, they would suggest the Qur'an affirms what it says in Acts: that "in (God) we live and breathe and have our being." (Acts 17:28) No

---

2. D,Andrews (2011)*Bismillah - Christian-Muslim Ramadan Reflections* Melbourne: Mosaic, p10

3. *Bismillah al rahman al Rahim* http://wahiduddin.net/words/bismillah.htm

4. W. Chittick 'The Islamic Notion of Mercy' *Huffington Post* July 12 2012 https://bit.ly/3SGvpWs

wonder many verses (in the Qur'an) say things like, *Allah* "is with you wherever you are." (57:4) [5]

According to Ibn Qayyum (1350 CE), *ra<u>h</u>man* describes the quality of limitless grace with which God embraces the whole of the world and all of those who dwell within it; while *rahim* describes the general embracing grace of God as it interacts with us in the particular circumstances of our lives—always proactive, compassionate, responsive.[6] And according to what Adis Duderija, has written in his presentation, we have "been tasked with a special ethical responsibility to embody and enact these Godlike ... attributes at both the level of individuals and societies seeking to create conditions that contribute to flourishing and well-being of all of God's creation."

Our world is in trouble; and religion, which was meant to make things better, has often made things worse. We do not suffer from the lack of religion, but from the lack of compassion. So, if we are to have any hope of not only surviving, but also thriving—and flourishing—we need to find a way to be able to care for ourselves, and for our world, once again. The radical spirituality of compassion that we remember when we recite the *Basmala* is not merely our best hope for true peace on the planet; it is our only hope for real peace on the planet.

Imam Jamal Rahman says—

> The art of invoking the *Basmala* in relating to others is, for me, epitomized in the sage advice offered by the fifteenth-century mystic Kabir. When we encounter someone who is harmful or offensive, of course we need to protect ourselves and prevent the abuse. But at the same time, we must make every effort to

---

[5]. W. Chittick 'The Islamic Notion of Mercy' *Huffington Post* July 12 2012 https://bit.ly/3SGvpWs

[6]. D. Andrews (2011)*Bismillah - Christian-Muslim Ramadan Reflections* Melbourne: Mosaic, p22

keep that person's essence in our heart. This may be hard to do, but we must remind ourselves again and again that we are fighting the antagonism, not the antagonist. Just the sheer energy of this awareness and discernment, as it informs our actions, has the power to shift heaven and earth. Remembering that God's essence is compassion and mercy, when we speak and act in justice we are expressing our consciousness of the highest form of compassion and mercy. In the name of God, in the spirit of *Basmala*, we must be compassionate to those in need, feeding the hungry and easing the pain of the afflicted.[7]

We need to constantly recite the *Basmala* and remember his 'mercy encompasses all'. The Prophet Muhammad (SWS) states: "Those who have no mercy on other human beings will not receive the mercy of God". 'It is important to note that in this *hadith* the word (for human beings) is *nas*, that is people, not just Muslims or believers of Islam'. 'Abdullah bin Umro bin Aas, says the Prophet (SWS) said: "Have mercy on those who are on earth, the One in heavens will have mercy on you".' *(Tirmidhi)*.

Maulana Wahiduddin Khan says "God has the same compassionate relationship with every man as a father has with all his children. Therefore, it is alien to the divine scheme of creation that this earthly plane should be marred by hatred and violence. It is God's most cherished desire that love should be returned for hatred and violence should be met with peace."

According to the Qur'an, paradise is God's neighbourhood and in this neighbourhood only those who have compassion—living in a way that (their) actions are of benefit (*maslaha*) to others—will find

---

[7]. Sheikh Jamal Rahman in Pastor Don Mackenzie, Rabbi Ted Falcon, and Sheikh Jamal Rahman, *'Getting to the Heart of Interfaith: The Eye-Opening, Hope-Filled Friendship of a Pastor, a Rabbi & an Imam'*, SkyLight Paths 2009, p69-73

acceptance'.[8] This is only possible if we do not react with hatred for hatred and repay violence with violence. And this is only possible if we immerse ourselves in the spirit of the *Basmala*, let it to saturate our mind and shape our emotions and so be able to 'embody Godlike attributes' in our actions and interactions.

Not everyone will feel comfortable with trying a reflective *sufi* way of allowing the *Basmala* to saturate their mind and shape their emotions, but we would invite all those who would feel comfortable doing so to immerse their mind and emotions in the *Basmala*, not simply reciting the *Bismillah* by rote, but intentionally saying the *Bismillah* in their heart and making the *Bismillah* the prayer of their heart.

We would invite everyone to make time and space to:

- Sit in a comfortable position.
- Ask God to put you in touch with the Spirit of the *Bismillah*.
- Close your eyes, and breathe in and out slowly, rhythmically.
- Breathe in and say '*Bismillah*' focusing on the name of God.
- Breathe out and say '*ir-Rahman ir-Rahim*' reflecting on God's mercy.
- Do this aloud to start with. Again and again. Increasingly slowly, softly.
- Take it into your heart. Pray it silently by heart as your heart prayer.
- Be aware of what you feel.
- Allow yourself to feel embraced by the mercy of God.
- Feel the mercy of God that embraces those whom you love.
- Feel the mercy of God that embraces even those you don't love.
- Imagine acting towards all people, with mercy and grace.
- Pray the *Bismillah* repeatedly, inhaling the *Bismillah* with every breath, pray that you might embody the *Bismillah* with

---

8. Maulana Wahiduddin Khan, *The Prophet of Peace*, (Penguin New Delhi 2009), 16.

every beat of your heart, through every vein in your head, your hands, and your feet, *"Bismillah ir-Rahman ir-Rahim!"*

Having learnt to make this the prayer of our heart we need to pray the *Bismillah,* not only at the beginning and end of the day, but also in times of crisis, in the nanoseconds between action and reaction, to saturate our mind and shape our emotions with mercy and grace and enable ourselves to "embody Godlike attributes" in our responses.

NURTURANT RELIGION FOR A BETTER WORLD

JOHN SANDERS, Professor Emeritus, Hendrix College,
for more information see www.DrJohnsanders.com.

I was having a discussion with a family member about some social issues when they said, "Stop. Before we go on, I need to know if you affirm any moral standards." I was shocked. Of course, I have moral standards! How could my relative question this? Christians in North America are deeply divided over theological, social, and political issues. Family members look at one another in disbelief, thinking that the other person's values are seriously wrongheaded. Unfortunately, this scene is found around the world and in other religions as well. When I presented this material to faculty and students at a university in Tehran, the response was an emphatic, "Yes! That is our experience as well."

I believe the best overall explanation for this great divide comes from social scientists who talk about two major value systems that orient ways of life: Nurturant and Authoritative. These two models represent distinct ways of living and relating that result in proponents of each side believing they live properly while the other is fundamentally wrong. For over thirty years, political scientists have used four questions to identify these two types. The questions pertain to four sets of characteristics people prefer in children. Please select the ones in each pairing you prefer.

- Independence or Respect for Elders
- Good Manners or Curiosity
- Well Behaved or Being Considerate
- Self-Reliance or Obedience

Those who choose independence, curiosity, being considerate, and self-reliance are strongly Nurturant. Those who select respect for elders, good manners, well behaved, and obedience are strongly Authoritative. Of course, there are people who select some from each category and so will bear less of a family resemblance to the prototypical Nurturant or Authoritative types, but this chapter focuses on those who select three to four characteristics of the Nurturant or Authoritative model. Researchers call these four questions their Rosetta Stone and use them in the World Values Survey of 108 countries representing 90% of the world's population.

The answers to the questions accurately predict the types of books, movies, and vehicles you prefer. More significantly, they indicate your stances on a host of political and social issues, such as whether women should have a role in the public sphere.[1] The core values and approach to justice in each way of life differ sharply. Here is a summary of the two models.

Nurturants

1. Core values: empathy, cooperation, perspective taking, the importance of community, and cognitive openness (the need for nuance and humility in truth claims).
2. Justice means making sure that all people have a solid opportunity to fulfill their potential in life. All should share the goods and services of society.

---

[1]. On the social issues as well as which pets each type prefers, see Marc Hetherington and Jonathan Weiler. *Prius or Pickup? How the Answers to Four Simple Questions Explain America's Great Divide*. Boston: Houghton Mifflin Harcourt, 2018.

Authoritatives
1. Core Values: obedience to rules, maintaining social order, individual responsibility, and cognitive closure (black-and-white thinking and certainty in truth claims).
2. Justice means getting what you deserve. If you follow the rules, then you deserve a reward. If you break the rules, then you deserve punishment.

My book, *Embracing Prodigals: Overcoming Authoritative Religion by Embracing Jesus' Nurturing Grace,* uses these two cognitive models to explain the polarization in American Christianity regarding many religious teachings and social issues. The core values and definition of justice each model employs motivate proponents to adopt very different views on religious and social topics such as God, hell, and democracy. Muslims and Christians in other countries can use these as a guide to identify the polarizations in their contexts.

God
Nurturant view of God:
- God has high expectations for the way we should live. God first manifests acceptance to get us to change the way we live.
- Divine justice seeks to enable all people to flourish.
- God loves/cares for everyone regardless of their faults, including those outside the religious community.
- God takes human concerns into account (such as prayer).
- Those who believe in the Nurturing God describe God as forgiving, gracious, loving, accepting, not controlling, helping, caring, compassionate, generous, merciful, and tolerant.

Authoritative view of God:
- We must first change, then God will accept us.

- Divine justice gives everyone what they deserve: if they follow the rules, then they can go to heaven. If they disobey and stray from the straight path, then they go to hell.
- God loves the Authoritative religious community and hates others.
- God does not take human concerns into account (such as prayer).
- Those who affirm the Authoritative God describe God as critical, punishing, judging, stern, wrathful, damning, disapproving, controlling, rigid, strict, and unforgiving.

A major stream of Authoritative religion in both Christianity and Islam is divine determinism—the view that God micromanages each detail of our lives such that everything that happens is part of God's blueprint. God does not accept input from us in prayer. We are supposed to follow God and be obedient to the supreme authority. According to this view, God installs specific people to lead our religious and political institutions. Their leadership style is the same as God's: they demand absolute obedience. Disobeying Authoritative religious or political leaders is the same as disobeying God. Even asking questions is not permitted. Authoritative systems are often abusive to people.

The God of Nurturant religion is quite different. God takes our concerns into account and does not say, "It is my way or the highway." God empowers us by showing grace and compassion. God provides wisdom for how to navigate our lives. God does not determine the leaders of religious and political institutions. God lets us make those decisions while seeking to persuade us regarding the best options. God provides a model for how human leaders should treat others. Typically, this means that leaders seek to listen to those in their charge and allow for questions.

Philosophers speak of God's "great making" properties. Often, this involves ideas such as God is never influenced by others (strong impassibility), and that God cannot change in any respect (strong immutability). However, if one begins with the values of Jesus, different "great making" properties can be selected, such as compassion and grace. For Islam, consider the *Bismillah*. Each surah of the Qur'an begins, "In the name of God the compassionate, the merciful." I suggest that compassion and mercy are superior "great making" properties to unchangeability. In addition, consider some of the ninety-nine names of God, such as forgiving, patient, guide, and *Al-Mujeeb* ("the responsive one"). These ideas cohere well with open and relational theology. A God with compassion who forgives those who stray from the path is greater than the deity who tightly controls everything we do and who lacks compassion.

Sin

Nurturants frame sin in relational terms—it is about harming and breaking relationships.

Authoritatives think of sin as breaking rules that require punishment. God hates those who disobey God's commandments.

Forgiveness

For Nurturants, God initiates forgiveness and uses it to motivate change. God shows us mercy, grace, and compassion to empower us to change our lives. God is well aware that we have problems, but instead of condemning us, God showers compassion on us. Ask yourself when you are most willing to change: when you are renounced or when you feel embraced?

For Authoritatives, humans must first change, then God will accept them. God has provided the rules by which to live. If you want divine acceptance, then follow the rules.

Does God extend salvation to non-believers?

Authoritatives say no. God gave the rules of salvation! Heaven is restricted to those who follow the divine instructions, the rest get hell. This is justice because God gives each what they deserve.

Nurturants says yes. They have several different views, including

1. inclusivism (God accepts those who respond positively to the work of God in their lives and
2. postmortem opportunity (God keeps pursuing people even after death).[2]

Hell

For Authoritatives, hell is eternal conscious punishment. People are aware of their torment, and it lasts forever. God locks the gates of hell from the outside to keep people from escaping. Divine justice means giving people exactly what they deserve. If they obeyed God's rules, then they go to heaven. If they disobeyed God, then they deserve hell.

Nurturants find an eternal torture chamber incompatible with God's love and justice. What purpose does punishing people forever accomplish except vindictiveness? The purpose of judgment is to transform people—restorative justice. Some hold that the gates of hell are locked from the inside by the people themselves. They prefer views such as

1. annihilation (those who reject God cease to exist) and
2. universal salvation, in which hell is restorative in that it seeks to restore the person to God so the person may flourish.

The Bible and the Qur'an

Nurturants see sacred texts as tools of grace to shape our communities. They are an invitation to a way of life, not a list of rules to memorize. The religious community is open to using the best human reasoning in dialog with sacred texts.

---

[2]. See Mohammad Khalil, *Islam and the Fate of the Others* (Oxford, 2012) and Sanders, *No Other Name* (Eerdmans, 1992).

Authoritatives see sacred texts as a rulebook for how to live. The rules are absolutes that cannot be questioned. Follow the rules, and life turns out well for you. Sacred texts always have priority over human reasoning.

Women

In church life, Nurturants tend to allow women to be in leadership positions, including being a priest or pastor. They believe that God has been working for thousands of years to promote women to full equality in religious life.

Authoritatives tend to hold that women must be subject to male authorities in both the family and the church. They cannot be leaders in either setting. In addition, Authoritatives argue that God primarily has "male" characteristics such as being stern, strict, and unforgiving. Some Authoritatives accuse Nurturant thinkers, such as me, of attributing "feminine" characteristics to God, such as mercy and kindness. However, characteristics such as unforgiving or mercy are neither male nor female. After all, Jesus was merciful and forgiving.

Cognitive Styles

- Nurturants believe it is virtuous to foster dialogue, perspective taking, empathy for others, and tolerance. Authoritatives do not value perspective taking. The only reason to learn the position of opponents is to know why they are wrong.
- Nurturants practice a "pilgrim" theology that is always on the journey and thus open to changes. God guides on the journey, but there are often several good routes from which to choose. God helps us adapt as new situations arise. Authoritatives prefer a "fortress" theology where everything is already settled, and you defend it against your enemies.
- Nurturants use epistemic humility in their truth claims even while they argue for a particular position. Nuance and qualification

are important. Authoritatives tend to hold their views with absolute certainty. They prefer black-and-white thinking without the need of qualifications.
- Though Nurturants reject some positions, usually there is a constrained pluralism of acceptable views on a topic. For instance, they reject views about hell, such as eternal conscious torment and may prefer hopeful universal salvation to the annihilation view, yet they allow for both views to be held in the religious community. Authoritatives score high on what psychologists call the "defensive theology scale." There is only one correct view, and if you do not affirm it, then you must be removed from the community. They do not like people asking questions about religious doctrines. They often ask: "What if you are wrong?" The implication is that God punishes those who hold different beliefs.
- Nurturants affirm the importance of dialogue and usually are willing to compromise. Authoritatives place little value on dialogue and see compromise as selling out. You must affirm the single correct view, or you will suffer the consequences.

Social and Political Issues.
- The different views on hell correspond to different approaches to criminal punishment. Authoritatives say we must be "tough on crime," espouse the death penalty, and generally want to lock up criminals and throw away the key (as God does to people in hell). Nurturants seek to restore the offender to the community because the purpose of judgment is to get people to change. This approach was enacted by the Truth and Justice Commission in South Africa after apartheid.
- In America, there are huge income and wealth gaps, particularly along racial lines. Authoritatives claim that Whites deserve higher incomes and more net worth because they work

harder. They believe everyone has adequate opportunities today. If you are not successful, blame yourself, not the system. Poverty would be abolished if people simply worked harder. They criticize Black Christians for relying on social programs instead of individual effort and for blaming institutions instead of themselves for their situation. Authoritatives who are poor believe that God is angry with them and so punishes their sins with low income. Religious Nurturants believe the government should change economic laws to ensure that everyone can fulfill their potential. Yes, individuals need to take initiative and work hard, but systems such as education, housing, and banking also play a key role in our lives and these systems can be designed in ways that help some while hampering others. Nurturants believe that saying the solution lies simply in working harder is like telling the folks on the Titanic to bail faster with their thimbles.

- Nurturants believe that just like good roads and schools, health care should be provided to all. Universal health care provides the freedom for people to flourish. Authoritatives think health care is a commodity like cars and TVs. Only the successful deserve it. If you cannot afford good health insurance, that is your fault.
- Nurturants prefer democratic or shared governance. They favor deliberative discourse and seek to ensure that all people have a voice in decisions. Authoritatives favor autocratic leaders. Nurturants say it is important for a democracy to (1) protect the rights of those with unpopular views, (2) protect the rights of news organizations to criticize political leaders, and (3) the right of nonviolent protest. Authoritatives tend to disagree. Many desire a "strong" political leader who can defy Congress and bypass elections. In many countries today, Authorities set the rules for elections so that only they can be elected.

Is One Way of Life Better Than the Other?

So far, I have shown that the underlying values lead to very different doctrines and stances on social issues, but is one approach any better than the other? Nurturant Christians can appeal to the life and teachings of Jesus, who lavished mercy and grace on those who did not deserve it. He empowered them to change by first showing love and acceptance. Jesus exemplified Nurturant values and taught that God relates to us in Nurturant ways.[3] Nurturant Muslims can appeal to passages in the Qur'an, the Hadith, and other resources to make the case that Nurturant values are what God desires in our lives.

Aside from religious sources, social science research provides significant evidence that Nurturant values promote a better way of life for both individuals and communities.[4] Here are a few of the findings.

- Studies from various countries with diverse cultures, such as China, Pakistan, and Australia, indicate that children raised by Nurturing parents and educators exhibit greater degrees of self-reliance, prosocial behavior, confidence in social settings, motivation to achieve, cheerfulness, self-control, and less substance abuse.
- Those who believe God is Nurturing are more likely to help others, including those who are religiously different. They are more cooperative, agreeable, and have better social relationships.
- Nurturants have significantly higher levels of conviction that their life has meaning, greater life satisfaction, and have less loneliness. They are less dogmatic, have higher self-esteem along with significantly less depression, general anxiety, and obsessive compulsion.

---

3. See Sanders *Embracing Prodigals* pages 16-26.
4. For references to the research see John Sanders, *Embracing Prodigals* pages 8-9, 41-45, and 118-119.

- Societies that are more Nurturant have lower death ra natural disasters and infectious diseases.

Conclusion

The polarization we experience in religion and politics is due to the embrace of very distinct sets of values. Nurturants and Authoritatives tend to affirm widely divergent doctrines and live according to drastically different cognitive styles. Each way of life makes sense to its proponents, while the other approach is deemed wrongheaded. Yet, the two ways of life are not equal.

Social science research shows that the Nurturant way of life leads to more well-functioning children, better mental health, and improved communities. In my mind, open and relational theologies can be key instruments in promoting Nurturant religion due to the way they understand how God works with us. God is open to us and engages in give-and-take relationships. God shows mercy and forgiveness when we do not deserve it. God guides and empowers without controlling us. An open and relational God shows us how to walk the path of life. A path that leads to human flourishing for both individuals and societies.

NURTURANT AND AUTHORITATIVE VIEWS OF GOD:
In Conversation with John Sanders

SHABIR ALLY, President of the Islamic Information & Dawah Centre International (IslamInfo.com), Resident scholar of the TV show 'Let the Quran Speak' (QuranSpeaks.com) and Muslim Media Hub in Canada (MuslimMediaHub.com).

Dr. Sanders has shown a sharp contrast between the nurturant and authoritative views of God and the social impact of these views. I agree with almost everything that he presented. He has alluded to elements of the Muslim faith that could support a nurturant view, such as the name of God: al-Rahman (the Most Merciful).

My points of agreement with Dr. Sanders are several. If space allowed, I would have advanced a progressive view of God's embracing of prodigals, a view of the limited duration of hell and the salvation of non-Muslims, subjects which Dr. Sanders elaborated here with such eloquence. However, given the limited space, I prefer to address what I feel is at the crossroads between the nurturant and authoritative views: the question of predestination, a problem whose history within Christian circles Dr. Sanders traced so adequately elsewhere.[1] It remains for me to address this problem from a Muslim perspective.

---

1. See his essay, "Historical Considerations," in *The Openness of God*, ed. Clark Pinnock et al (Downers Grove, Illinois: InterVarsity Press, 1994) pp. 59-100.

Given its complexity, predestination needs to be addressed as thoroughly as possible. First, I must acknowledge that Muslims have always been torn between views on predestination and human freedom. However, as classically formulated, the faith opted for the predestinarian view. This formulation is reflected in Islamic law, exegesis, and theology, all of which find validation in hadith, which themselves developed in tandem with Muslim thought in the said fields.

The tension that Muslims felt between these two paradigms is reflected in a hadith according to which a non-Muslim child had died. The story involves Ayesha, respectfully referred to as the mother of the believers, and at the mention of whose name Sunni Muslims tend to say, "May God be pleased with her." She remarked affectionately that the deceased child was now one of the little birds in paradise. But the prophet Muhammad, on whom be peace, interjected. He explained that Allah created people designating them for Paradise or Hell before their conception.[2] From this hadith, it is clear that the child could have grown up to be a sinner and that God, knowing all things in advance, would treat the departed soul of the child in accordance with the foreknowledge of what the child would have done if allowed to reach maturity.

That God's foreknowledge underpins a deterministic universe became commonplace in Sunni Muslim theology, though this was not always the case. At one time, those now dubbed Qadarites argued for human freedom and divine justice as being predicated upon that concept. The Qadarites were followed by or evolved into the Mutazilites, the rationalists, whose rational approaches have survived more in Shiite Muslim circles than among Sunnis. Sunnites mostly went the way of Abul Hasan al-Ashari (d. 936 C.E). The latter had mastered Mutazilite thought but turned away from using rationality

---

2. Imam Muslim, *Sahih Muslim* trans. Abdul Hamid Siddiqi (Lahore: Sh. Muhammad Ashraf, 1976) Vol. 4, p. 1433; Book 31, hadith 6435.

as a determinant of truth. He became content with using rationality merely to defend the truth, which is known from hadith, or, more broadly, Muslim tradition.

If everything is predestined, why, according to al-Ashari, would the punishment of sinners be justified? Because, he says, sinners acquire the sin which God had already chalked out for them. The justification seems lame, but the Asharite school became the hallmark of Muslim scholarship into the Middle Ages. Muslims today struggle with the concept of divine determinism, with most Muslims sensing a problem with the doctrine. Muslim savants, sensing the doubts among the masses, tend to double down, insisting on the doctrine in sermons, fatwas, and treatises.

However, Muslims today can find a way out of this difficulty by looking more closely at the early evolution of Muslim thought. The earliest and most reliable document for Muslims in determining faith and practice is the Quran. The Quran no doubt has passages that can be interpreted in a deterministic manner. However, there are mitigating verses pointing to human freedom. For example, "Let those who wish to believe believe, and let those who wish to disbelieve disbelieve" (Quran 18:27). This points to human choice. Not only this verse but the Quran as a whole resounds with this message: people have the choice to believe or not.

It is true that the Quran uses the term *qadar* which acquired the meaning of predestination in Muslim theology.[3] But the term needs to mean only "a measure." The Quranic message is that God has measured out everything. This could mean that things are measured out in ranges. Hence, a person's lifespan, for example, could have been measured out in advance as a range. Thus, with proper diet, exercise,

---

3. For the range of meanings associated with *qadar*, see Israr Ahmad Khan, *Authentication of Hadith: Redefining the Criteria* (London: International Institute of Islamic Thought, 2010) pp. 141-43.

and advances in medical treatment, people could live relatively longer, provided that they neither exceed the prescribed range nor fall short of it. All of this would be within the *qadar,* the range of divine pre-measurement.

It is easy even for those who do not speak Arabic to appreciate that *qadar* does not mean predestination, at least in Quran 22:74. Leaving the word *qadar* untranslated for the moment, the verse faults non-believers because they do not *qadar* God with the *qadar* that God deserves. If qadar means predestination, the verse would be blaming non-believers for not predestining God as he deserves to be predestined! Rather, *qadar* here means "measure." Hence, according to *The Study Quran*, the verse means, "They did not measure God with his true measure."[4]

In sum, the Quran does not support the theory of absolute predestination. Though it presents God as being in control, God also maintains human freedom within broad controls.

But the hadith corpuses are more difficult to tweak towards establishing human freedom. These corpuses each commonly include a chapter on the subject chock full of snippets, like the one about the deceased child mentioned earlier, establishing absolute divine control of each person's outcome. Yet even these corpuses contain traditions that go against the grain in showing that things are not as predestined as the other traditions insist. For example, in *Sahih al-Bukhari,* widely regarded among Muslims as the most authentic collection of hadith, there is a hadith showing that there are two abodes predetermined for each person, one in heaven and the other in hell such that, in the end, residents of heaven will see their alternative place in hell which they would have occupied if they had done evil. Likewise, dwellers of

---

4. Syed Hossein Nasr, ed., *The Study Quran: A New Translation and Commentary* (NY: HarperCollins, 2015) p. 848.

hell will see their alternative place in heaven, which they would have occupied if they had done good.⁵

That hadith, clearly, is in line with the tenor of the Quran: do good and go to heaven; do bad and end up in hell. But many hadiths give the contrary position: that people will end up where God had predetermined that they will end up. And what of their deeds? Well, their deeds will follow what God had predetermined for them.

Yet even some of those hadiths, when studied carefully, reveal how the words of a reported saying of the prophet Muhammad, on whom be peace, could have been changed in Arabic by the tradents and in English by the translators.

Two competing versions of a certain hadith differ mainly in a single word: either it uses the word 'and' to conjoin heaven and hell, or it uses the word 'or' to disjoin the two abodes. The variation in the Arabic is probably due to a mistake in transmission, especially in the early, mostly oral, stage of transmission. One version of the hadith in question indicates that there are two places determined for each person: one in heaven; *and* one in hell, thus agreeing with the hadith cited above and leading to a non-fatalistic outlook.⁶ The same hadith, in a variation that supports determinism, indicates that a final place in heaven *or* hell has been predetermined for each human, implying that one destined for heaven cannot go somewhere else, whereas one destined for hell cannot escape that outcome.⁷ Unfortunately, the latter variant, disjoining the two abodes, allotting a single space to each person, thus favouring determinism, is the one championed by the evolved classical tradition.

It is interesting to see how the translator of Sahih al-Bukhari handles the two versions of this hadith. Where the disjunction is *wa* in

---

5. Al-Bukhari, *Sahih al-Bukhari*, trans. Muhammad Muhsin Khan (Medina: Islamic University, n.d.) vol. 8, pp. 372-73, book 76, #573.
6. Bukhari, vol. 6, nos. 469, 472, and 474.
7. Bukhari, vol. 6, no. 471, vol. 8, no. 602, and vol. 9, no. 642.

Arabic, the translator reasonably renders this as "or." But in the variant wherein the conjunction *wa* occurs, instead of rendering it "and" as any beginning student of Arabic might expect, here too, the translator uses the English disjunction "or." Thus, even the variant that clearly supports a non-deterministic view is tamed in translation to tout the deterministic view. Nonetheless, the other variant is still there in *Sahih al-Bukhari*, in the original Arabic, waiting to be reclaimed as a variant that goes against the grain of the tradents and, for this reason, is probably more authentic than its competitor.

If we allow our critical eye to return to the story of the deceased child, we can see that the hadith in that story is in two distinct parts. In the first part, Ayesha declared that the child is now a bird in paradise. In the second part, Muhammad[8] expresses caution about such a conclusion. Applying what we know about form-criticism in Biblical studies, the first part of this tradition, conceivably, could have circulated devoid of the second part, and thus the second part could have been appended later. If that is so, then Ayesha's conclusion would have been the only one: the child is in heaven. But then, someone thought it necessary to reverse that conclusion in order to support the then-developing predestinarian view.

In sum, the hadith corpuses developed at a time and in circles in which predestination was the accepted theory. Therefore, hadiths can be expected to support that view. Yet there are indications in the corpuses that stark predeterminism was not always the view among Muslims.

In fact, from historical studies, we know of the existence of the Qadarites, advocates of human freedom, and the Mutazilites, rationalists who rejected stark determinism.

---

8. Muslims dutifully ask God to bless Muhammad when they come across mention of his name.

Hence, Muslims today are not predestined to accept predestination as a necessary component of our faith. Rather, we can reclaim the balance between human freedom and divine control, allowing for such freedom within broad parameters.

If we can strike this balance, then we will be able to develop a nurturing theology. Knowing that God is nurturing, not micro-managing, will empower us to align ourselves with God's plans in nurturing and caring for creation.

Embracing a nurturing approach rather than an authoritative one will also have major social implications. Imagine a Muslim world with less authority and more egalitarianism; less monarchy, more democracy.

In conclusion, I applaud Dr. Sanders for his enlightening bifurcation between the nurturant and authoritative views. I feel that his discussion of determinism elsewhere had relevance here as a component of the authoritarian approach. Hence, I wanted to commend the nurturant view to Muslims with my explication of an Islamic view on the question of predestination. I hope that my humble contribution will be seen as a student's addendum to Dr. Sander's excellent essay.

It remains for me to also advance a progressive view on the temporality of hell, the salvation of non-Muslims, and God's embracing of prodigals. Perhaps another time.

BIRDS WITH WINGS OUTSPREAD:
Christianity, Islam and the Earth

CATHERINE KELLER, George T. Cobb Professor of Constructive Theology, Drew University Theological School, for more information, see www.catherineekeller.com.

———

In this planetarily stressed time: how heartening to be thinking together across Christian and Muslim perspectives.[1] We are therefore thinking "openly and relationally" across the earth.[2] That planetary context itself—precisely in its earthiness—demands new forms of religious attention. For it is now broadly understood that what we too blandly designate as climate change or global warming can no longer be treated as a string of exceptional emergencies. We have rather to do with an inescapable emergence, one that, in its planetarity, belongs at the center of religious and, therefore, interreligious concern. Of course, John B. Cobb, Jr got process theology there over half a century

---

[1]. An ancestor of this essay was published in this crucial anthology: *Nature and the Environment in Contemporary Religious Contexts,* edited Thomas Donlin-Smith and Muhammad Shafiq (Cambridge Scholars Publishing, 2018. The book is based on a conference organized by Professor Shafiq at the Hickey Center for Interfaith Studies and Dialogue: *Sacred Texts and Human Contexts: Nature and Environment in World Religions* March 23-25 2016

[2]. The worlds of process theology and of Christian thought owe much, and ever more, to the "open and relational" vision, practice and prolific authorship of Thomas Jay Oord.

ago, posing the intolerable question: Is It Too Late?[3] And as Jürgen Moltmann, leading theologian of the Reformed tradition and its major ecological voice, later would formulate the challenge concisely: "The so-called great world religions will only prove themselves to be 'world religions,' when they become earth religions and understand humanity as an integrated part of the planet earth."[4] Only thereby does a planetary width of solidarity, and with it, an earth-wide and earthy planetary solidarity, become possible. And only that possibility keeps hope alive: hope for the future of the human habitat.

Yet the world religions, particularly in their Abrahamic modes, cannot be called earth religions. They have outgrown much but not nearly enough of what we may call their ecophobia. They remain often nervous about their own earthiness, fearing it could lead to idolatrous nature-worship, pantheism, reductionism, atheism, materialism… And they remain—perhaps especially Christianity—divided in themselves, not just over ecology but over gender and sexuality, indeed over the whole range of social justice commitments, involving also the status of their own universal claims to truth. Perhaps therefore, we might, for the present discussion, think from this shared presumption: that the *planetarity* of a world religion no longer refers simply to the universality of its outreach, the globality of its truth claim. Planetarity signifies, at the same time, our ecological responsibility.

---

3. John B. Cobb, Jr., Is it Too Late? A Theology of Ecology. 1995 Environmental Ethics Books…..First published 1972, Bruce…. First book-length treatment in theology, religion or philosophy of the ecological problem.

4. Jürgen Moltmann, "Eine gemeinsame Religion der Erde (A Common Religion of the Earth): Weltreligionen in ükologischer Perspektive (World Religions in Ecological Perspective)," in *Verlag Otto Lembeck* 10/1605, "Okumenische Rundschau" (2011), 26 (my translation). As discussed in my *Cloud of the Impossible: Negative Theology and Planetary Entanglement* (New York: Columbia University Press, 2014), 279-80. ADD English Version. A helpful critique points out that the problem is not between Christians and other religions but between Christians on opposite sides of the progressive/liberal and conservative/traditional spectrum.

http://www.scielo.org.za/scielo.php?script=sci_arttext&pid=S0259-94222020000 100064

So, for example, to strengthen this ability to respond, many Christians and Jews—if not the conservative ones—have regular recourse to Genesis 1. After all, what God declares "very good" is not the exceptional human, but rather "everything that God had made" [1.31]. "Everything" signifies the entire Genesis collective, which Lynn White called "a. spiritual democracy of all God's creatures." He was in 1966 already pushing against Christian and secular anthropocentrism.[5] And in the process world, we recall Whitehead's claim: "We find ourselves in a buzzing world, amid a democracy of fellow creatures…" He is, of course, not confronting climate change but the common sense metaphysics of a world of "solitary substances…"And if we now lean into that democracy as anti-exceptionalist in its ecology, Whitehead also delivers its theology: "God is not to be treated as an exception to all metaphysical principles, invoked to save their collapse." God is rather "their chief exemplification."[6] We may worry less now about the collapse of a commonsense substance metaphysics than of the world it shaped. But that common sense still trends exceptionalist—at the level of the species, let alone nation or theology. So let us recall that "to except" means originally "to take out." And that exceptionalism is 'taking out' our shared future. In the eco-theological alternative, then, the biblical *imago dei* does not mark us humans as the *exception* to the creaturely collective; rather, we arise as its communicative *exemplification*.[7]

---

5. Lynn Townsend White, Jr. "The Historical Roots of our Ecologic Crisis" Science 155, no. 3767 (1967). His father (Lynn Townsend White) was a Presbyterian minister and professor of Christian social ethics.
See Matthew T. Riley, "A Spiritual Democracy of All God's Creatures: Ecotheology and the Animals of Lynn White Jr." in *Divinanimality: Animal Theory, Creaturely Theology*, Edited by Stephen D. Moore. Drew Transdisciplinary Theological Colloquium 2011. (NYC: Fordham University Press, 2014).
6. Alfred North Whitehead Process & Reality: An Essay in Cosmology (Free Press, 1978 [1929] 50; 343.
7. I've worked elsewhere with the distinction of exceptionalism and exemplarity, esp. in *A Political Theology of the Earth*, Columbia 2018.

In our exemplarity lies our great diversity—creaturely and religious. As it happens, those theologies that emphasize the gift of creaturely diversity tend also to recognize religious diversity as a gift. Interfaith relations and ecological relations both express a deep, constitutive relationalism. A main reason I chose to study with John Cobb was that he teaches that it is not just secular liberalism that calls Christians to be open to learning from other religions. As the cosmic logos, Christ is calling us: not just to the *conversion* of others, and on the other hand, not just to *conversation*, but to "mutual transformation."[8] But even we pluralist Christians have not gone far in recognizing how much we can learn from our Abrahamic sibling Islam on many fronts. And I will emphasize here: we have not realized how Islam can help us overcome our own Western and Christian forms of anthropocentrism.

The Islamic Declaration on Global Climate Change (2015) offers one particularly inviting portal into such conversation: "If we each offer the best of our respective traditions, we may yet see a way through our difficulties."[9] Consider in that spirit this citation it lifts up from the Qur'an: "*No living creature is there moving on the earth, no bird flying on its two wings, but they are communities like you*" [6.38]. The elegant evocation of the importance of animal communities does not contradict the Bible but adds something of crucial importance: birds, bees, and bears are not just creatures but communities. Like humans! Thus, Mohammad reveals in all animals a startling register of connective complexity and social dignity. And at the same time, he undoes the common sense of mere separate entities: each is a relational creature.

And now consider the following verse of the Qur'an: "*Surely the creation of the heavens and the earth is something greater than the creation*

---

8. John B. Coob, Jr. *Christ in a Pluralistic Age* Westminster Press, 1975
9. http://islamicclimatedeclaration.org/islamic-declaration-on-global-climate-change/

of humankind, but most of humankind do not know [this truth]" [40.57].
I know of no sacred text of Christianity that so directly and pointedly names the whole cosmic context as both *greater* than the human—and as, for the most part, *unrecognized* as such. This sense of cosmological mystery does not diminish human distinctiveness. In no way does it underplay the difference. The text beautifully undermines not human difference but human exceptionalism. And it thereby seeks a new sense of tawhid, the oneness of Allah that fosters a unity of peace, not homogeneity. It forges what Abdul Asiz Said and Nathan Funk call "peace in Islam" as "ecology of the spirit."[10]

Muslim environmentalists, such as in this case Ibrahim Ozdemir, also stress the following remarkable passage: *"Don't you see that it is God Whose praises all beings in the heavens and on earth do celebrate, and the birds with wings outspread? Each one knows its own mode of prayer and praise. (And God knows well all that they do.)"* [24:41-42][11]

If I may respond to that rhetorical question: Do we (Christians in particular) not see how this text says something terribly fresh? It echoes old Hebrew psalms of trees clapping their hands, of valleys, shouting and singing together for joy," all the earth worships you."[12]—profoundly non-anthropocentric metaphors of an earthy faith. Metaphors readily jilted to the background of most Christian worship. But the Islamic text seems to go a bit further, making explicit claims that all beings *pray*. This celebratory teaching surely undermines the human claim to be the exception before God. And it thereby frees prayer itself from anthropocentric talktalktalk. It can

---

10. Abdul Aziz Said and Nathan C. Funk, "Peace in Islam: An Ecology of the Spirit," in *Islam and Ecology: A Bestowed Trust,* edited by Richard C. Foltz, Frederick M. Denny, and Azizan Baharuddin (Cambridge, MA: Harvard University Press, 2003). See also S. Nomanul Haq, "Islam and Ecology: Toward Retrieval and Reconstruction." Daedalus Fall 2001.
11. Ibrahim Ozdemir, "Toward an Understanding of Environmental Ethics from a Qur'anic Perspective," in *Islam and Ecology: A Bestowed Trust.*
12. Ps 65.13; 66.4

then serve as both a means to and an expression of cosmic attunement. Whiteheadians might say: yes, every actual occasion is potentially attuned to the divine lure. So might Islam even now help us to relearn such attunement from the birds—as we spread our wings to face the mass extinctions and other endless consequences of our own species' exceptionalist destructiveness?

Put ontologically, the alternative to sovereign exceptionalism can be couched as "entangled difference."[13] Our differences do not get diminished by relation. Rather, they get emphasized—sometimes exaggerated, sometimes opposed—within the webs of our manifold entanglements. Such relationality echoes that of quantum entanglement, the physics that attests to what Karen Barad calls the "intra-activity" of all things: already at the minimal material level of an electron and across any measurable distance whatsoever.[14] Quantum entanglement offers an elemental illustration of our "open and relational" universe. And in no small measure, Whitehead was inspired to shift his work from mathematics to cosmology by the shock of the quantum theory—with its pulsations of micro-events in vastly unfolding energy fields.[15] Recognizing that relations are intrinsic to the relata, their entangled difference means that however much we differentiate, decide and separate, we can never quite *extricate*. Indeed, at the most basic material level, we remain ontologically, unexceptionally, nonseparable—except by a "fallacy of misplaced concreteness—from our whole universe of relations.

---

13. C. Keller, *Cloud of the Impossible: Negative Theology and Planetary Entanglement* (Columbia, NYC: 2015)

14. Karen Barad, "Posthumanist Performativity: Toward an Understanding of How Matter Comes to Matter," *Signs: Journal of Women in Culture and Society* 28, no. 3 (Spring 2003): 801-831. For an extended discussion of Barad's work and more generally of the entanglement of quantum physics and negative theology see "Spooky Entanglements: The Physics of Nonseparability," in my *Cloud of the Impossible*, chapter 4.

15. https://www.fordhampress.com/9780823250127/quantum-mechanics-and-the-philosophy-of-alfred-north-whitehead/ use?

Webs within webs of connectivity: each creature a community, each species a community of communities, as Mohammad prophetically signaled. This nonseparability keeps us thinking, perhaps even praying, cosmically. And the cosmos now turns us back to face our own planet and its ecology of badly frayed relations—including those within and between our religious traditions. Repressed or recognized, entangled difference applies as much to interfaith exchange as it does to intercreaturely integrity. Do I become less Christian if I learn more from Islam? Or rather, does my Christianity just get more complicated—*com-plicans*, folding together—with the faiths of others. It was folded together with Judaism and with Hellenism from the start. Every new dialogue is a folding, an enfolding, and an unfolding of difference. Not a homogenization or a division, if it is an honest exchange, but a differentiation.

In Christianity, this positively complicating insight already seems to have been realized with particular relevance to the present discussion by the 15th-century Nicholas of Cusa. Based on a journey to Constantinople, he studied the Qu'ran and called—in an Islamophobic epoch—for a religious peace derived from shared awareness of divine mystery. He is one of the great voices of so-called negative or apophatic theology—the rigorous practice of knowing the limits and the dark-outs of our knowledge.[16] In *De Pace Fides*, he argues that because no religion can "know" God, none can exclude the possible truths of the others. So he calls not for the conversion of all to Christianity but "through Wisdom" hopes for a peaceful coexistence of the different faiths as "*religio una in rituum variatate*" (one religion in multiple rites). Christianity is thereby read as a "rite," not as its own religion. Startlingly for his time and in faithful service as a Cardinal to a Pope who would launch a new crusade in response

---

16. See my chapter on Nicholas of Cusa in *Cloud of the Impossible*—a phrase itself borrowed from his writing.

to the catastrophic Ottoman defeat of Constantinople, Cusa wrote: "Because of religion many take up arms against each other and by their power either force men to renounce their long-practiced tradition or inflict death on them." [17] And he corresponded with his friend Juan de Segovia about the need for a responsible translation of the Koran.[18] They even discussed the possibility of a conference as an alternative to another crusade. That alternative sadly remained an abstraction.

In my *Cloud of the Impossible*, I borrow from Cusa a mystical language of enfolding and unfolding: the divine *complicatio* and *explicatio*. No one, and no one religion, cognitively masters God. It is impossible: the divine infinity is everywhere and therefore unfolds in cosmic diversity. This is an ancestral theological vision of boundless cosmic connectivity: "all things are in all things." And "since the universe is contracted in each actual existing thing, it is obvious that God, who is in the universe, is in each thing, and each actual thing is immediately in God, as is the universe."[19] And so there necessarily also unfold multiply diverse, not simply separable religious Ways. This apophatic theology—claiming not to "know" but to "conjecture"— played a role also in the development of natural science (Copernicus cites Cusa, for example.)[20] Although most process theologians evince little interest in the apophatic, Cusa (as my Cloud insists) offers a magnificent cosmological antecedent for the mutual immanence of process relations and our multi-scaled entanglement in the universe,

---

17. *Cloud,* 242
18. See Jesse Mann "Throwing the Book at Them: Juan De Segovia's Use of the Quran" in Revista Espanola de Philosophia Medieval https://www.academia.edu/39863027/Jesse_D_Mann
19. Nicholas of Cusa "On Learned Ignorance," in *Nicholas of Cusa: Selected Spiritual Writings* (Paulist Press: Mahway, 1997), 140.
20. Cusa precedes natural science by a century in recognizing that the earth is not the center of the universe, indeed that the universe has no center—except the divinity whose "center is everywhere and circumference nowhere." And by longer than that in understanding that every location and characterization takes place in a boundless field of interdependent relativities. See *Cloud* 117-20

in the earth, and in each other. Each other—creature. It is not that the good Cardinal offers a flawless antecedent for interfaith or ecological work, let alone any pure exception from Christian supremacism. But he exemplifies a radically relational and ecological potentiality deep in Christianity. In this early and clearly proto-process vision, a cosmology of radical relation goes hand in hand with a theology of peaceful relation between "rites."

We surely need the historical reverberation of such ancestral voices more than only scriptural. Otherwise, we cannot correct from within the Christianity that mutes the deep terrestrial connections—intercreaturely and interreligious. We need ancestral help in holding Christology responsible to the ecumene: the *oikos*, "home," root of ecu-menism and eco-logy, roots us into deep and earthy, truly home planet, solidarity. Openly and relationally. Socially and politically. And neither, ever, without complications.

Of course, the tensions between Christianity and Islam—or any other faith—come readily to a head over the status of Jesus. Here suffice it to say (a) that for Islam, Jesus as the Christ means more than he does for many serious Christians. That is, Isa bin Mariam (Jesus, son of Mary) is understood not just as a great prophet but as Messiah, miracle worker, son of a virgin, and messenger of God. Much historical-critical Christianity would fully acquiesce in that Christology. But also, those many more Christians who remain Christocentric without demanding that others convert-or-go-to-hell can surely honor that Muslim account of Jesus. And process Christians can advance our own quite congruent process Christology. After all, Whitehead does not read even God (let alone Christ) as "the supreme exception to all metaphysical principles…" Such as the principles of interdependence in dynamic becoming. Instead, God is "their chief exemplification."

Liberated from the Christian supremacist history of the exceptionalisms, we may understand Jesus as an embodiment of a love that seeks to materialize in all creatures. Far from competing with other expressions of spirituality, it is interested in them. We can even have recourse to the medieval tradition of Christ, the *exemplar*. Indeed, with no supersessionist triumphalism, we can claim him as the primary known exemplar among humans of a metaphysics of transformative relationality. The Whiteheadian exemplarism is arguably more faithful to the sacred texts than any Christian exceptionalism. What of John 14.6, you might ask: "I am the way, and the truth and the life." This verse, the bane of religious pluralism, gets routinely mispronounced as: *I am THE way, THE truth, serves as the bane....* In context, however, the gospel has nothing to do with other religions. Jesus was saying to his disciples, who were expressing fear of losing their way if he died, that their lives were already entangled in his life, in his way. They will not get lost. And while, of course, Christ is for even his least exclusivist followers "the way"—that is the way of radical hospitality and respect for the stranger, a way that would surely require respectful interfaith exchange.

And now that love-way would also require of Christians what I have elsewhere called a political theology of the earth.[21] For as I write, speaking of politics, the Supreme Court has upheld the third Muslim Ban, instated by President Trump. And so surely the political urgency of struggles against Islamophobia can and must be held in relation to the ecumenism of struggles against ecological collapse. (Even without here getting into the thorny relevance of the relation to ecotheology of the carbon contributions of US and Arab oil!)

Given so many competing struggles across the planet (as I write, and even more, I fear, as you read): might we still hope that we can shift climate catastrophe into catalyst? Hope: that has not the self-assurance of optimism. Without hope, nothing—*nihil*, nihilism. Without it, we surrender to the seductions of consumerism, the intensities of more

---

21. Catherine Keller, *Political Theology of the Earth: Our Planetary Emergency and the Struggle for a New Public* (New York: Columbia, 2019).

immediate crises, or the paralysis of despair. But what does hope hope *for*? Hope as a normative value arises from the biblical text. It comes from the prophetic tradition of the novum: "Behold, I am doing a new thing, now it springs forth, do you not perceive it?"(Is. 43.19) So the novum must not be confused with the exception, which will only prove the hopeless rule of the same old sovereignties. This hope is for a transformation of the atmosphere and the earth (*hashamayin et ha eretz*), a radical renewal of the whole Genesis collective. And it requires our collaboration: as Karl Barth nailed it: "hope comes in taking the next step."[22]

The great textual danger that we who have some voice among the *Abrahamisms* must address may be passivity mistaken for faith: reliance on all-controlling power to intervene (in the miraculous exception). So then, when we trash the earth, that too, somehow serves God's mysterious will. Then our hope is just for a supernatural heaven, not the renewed heavens and earth. Such is the hope we must hope against. It mistakes eschatology for escape from the creation. As the great theologian of hope puts it, "We have no need to leave this world behind in order to look for God in a world to come. We only need to enter this world with its beauties and terrors, for God is already there. God waits for us through everything that God has created, and speaks to us through all of the creatures."[23]

The Christianity that can hear God's creative speech in all creatures can also hear it in all of the earth's religions. Perhaps the very dynamism of hope rests here: that to face the climate crisis together, we require, we step toward, a new solidarity of earth-wide ecumenism. The *oikos* of ecology and of ecumene can only together overcome the control of the earth-wasting global *eco*nomy. Our shared earth home

---

22. Karl Barth, *Church Dogmatics* IV, 3 [33], in *Church Dogmatics: A Selection with Introduction by Helmut Gollwitzer* (Louisville: Westminster John Knox, 1994), 82.
23. Jürgen Moltmann, *The Living God and the Fullness of Life* (Louisville, KY: Westminster John Knox Press, 2015), 171.

demands a triple oikos: of ecological, ecumenical, and responsibly economic cohabitation. And to sustain that life-or-death cooperation is to make possible, not certain but possible—the convivial future the Abrahamic faiths all envision.

Conviviality, as the living together in the togetherness of all creatures, requires something more than ethical solidarity. Something like attraction: the feeling of earth's beauty. Let this reflection, therefore, end with the conclusion of the Islamic Declaration on … Climate Change. It speaks for itself—and takes the form of a Hadīth narrated by the 7th century Abu Sa'īd Al-Khudrī:

"We bear in mind the words of our Prophet (peace and blessings be upon him): The world is sweet and verdant, and verily Allah has made you stewards in it, and He sees how you acquit yourselves."[24]

The sweet greenness of the world, the sensual delight—what a joyous reframing of our stewardship. The whole misreading of the biblical "dominion" for purposes of domination and exploitation dissipates in a fragrant breeze. Might Islam thus intensify the aesthetic motivation for eco-social solidarity? So the nation's leading ecoactivist Bill McKibben (a United Methodist), writes from Vermont during this month's shocking floods: "The crazily raging river a quarter mile from my door scares me, but it also makes me think how stunning it is in its usual form. This planet remains stirringly beautiful, and that beauty must be one of the things that moves us to act."[25]

As one of the co-authors of the Islamic Declaration, Saffet Catovic, put it later, in aptly down-to-earth language: "With this climate change issue, especially these last two years, religious leaders

---

[24]. Both the Islamic Declaration on Climate 2015 and the Joint Statement for COP26 in Glasgow cite this text. http://islamicclimatedeclaration.org/islamic-declaration-on-global-climate-change/

https://www.ifees.org.uk/wp-content/uploads/2021/10/cop26-muslim-statement.pdf

[25]. https://mail.google.com/mail/u/0/#inbox/FMfcgzGtvsZCskrhrPSnRkMVgpwqnWQc

around the world are not praying against each other, they're praying with one another for a common cause. Because the realization has set in that we're gonna have nothing left."[26]

In the hope of creative interaction between faiths for the sake of our common home, may we pray with one another now: like birds with wings outspread.

---

[26]. http://www.pri.org/stories/2016-12-30/muslim-environmentalists-give-their-religion-and-their-mosques-fresh-coat-green. I report with great pride that Imam Catovic is currently a student in Drew University's Graduate Division of Religion.

INTERRELIGIOUS OPEN THEOLOGY AND HUMAN EXCEPTIONALISM:
In Conversation with Catherine Keller

PD Dr. JOHANNES GRÖSSL, Universität Würzburg.

Comparative theology always starts with the awareness that one's own religion has a *weakness*. One important weakness of Christianity, as stressed by Catherine Keller, is human exceptionalism. That God has created humans in God's own image is a core doctrine in Christianity, with important advantages, especially when it comes to the foundation of human rights and when establishing a model of revelation which focuses on dialog and not on mere submission.[1]

But the doctrine also has its downsides: A Godlike human being can see itself as disconnected from and superior to the rest of creation. We know an extreme form of this view in Gnostic and Neoplatonic traditions in Early Christianity: The Godlike element in us is supposed to be thought, reason, and pure spirit. The goal can only be overcoming one's physical attachments, becoming pure spirit, and overcoming the material world. But even though these extremes were rejected by mainstream Christian tradition, the idea that human nature is constituted mainly by cognitive abilities has been living on: Michelle Voss

---

[1]. See N. Vorster, Created in the Image of God. Understanding God's Relationship with Humanity, Eugene: Wipf and Stock 2011.

Roberts calls this the (misguided) *priority of the intellect*.[2] This priority has found its complement in large parts of Western Enlightenment philosophy, such as the work of Immanuel Kant who defended human exceptionalism based on human's capacity to reason and to make moral choices based upon reason.[3]

But did God create the universe solely for humans or for the evolvement of rational creatures? Some theologians (even myself in the past) argue like this: God created the world so that he can engage in a loving relationship with his creatures; a genuine loving relationship requires free will, and free will requires reason. As far as we know, reason and the ability to love, are only actualized in humanity. This argument implies that everything else—planets, ecosystems, plants, animals—are only there to serve the purpose of humanity.[4] As I understand it, in her pledge against human exceptionalism, Keller promotes the idea that non-human reality has its own dignity, or at least, that humanity is essentially embedded in non-human reality and thus has its dignity only in relation to the whole planet Earth.

---

2. Michelle Voss Robert shows how Thomas Aquinas has promoted the ratiocentric model in Christianity; see "Embodiment, Anthropology, and Comparison: Thinking-Feeling with Non-Dual Saivism", in *How to Do Comparative Theology*, ed. F. X. Clooney & K. v. Stosch, New York: Fordham University Press 2018, 137-163, 141-143.

3. Immanuel Kant, Anthropology from a Pragmatic Point of View, Cambridge University Press 2012, 15: "The fact that the human being can have the "I" in his representations raises him infinitely above all other living beings on earth. Because of this he is a person, and by virtue of the unity of consciousness through all changes that happen to him, one and the same person—i.e., through rank and dignity an entirely different being from things, such as irrational animals, with which one can do as one likes. This holds even when he cannot yet say 'I,' because he still has it in thoughts, just as all languages must think it when they speak in the first person, even if they do not have a special word to express this concept of 'I.' For this faculty (namely to think) is understanding."

4. Even if there are other intelligent species on other planets, the same theological problem arises regarding their eco-systems, as long as they include non-rational lifeforms.

I believe there is a link between a teleological theory of creation out of love and eco-theology, since love—and this is where some personal theists are mistaken—is also, but not only realized in loving relationships between personal agents. Clark Pinnock, although a famous promoter of open theism, accepts that there are multiple reasons for God to create. On the one hand he says that the "foundation of the significance of our creaturely existence is the fact the God delights in us and wants a relationship with us."[5] On the other hand, he writes:

"But God is also delighted with it, as an artist who loves to express creativity. Creation gives God an occasion, as it were, to express his unsurpassability. God is able, by creating the world, to actualize his own potential: not the potential to be God, but the potential to be the creator of a non-divine world and the potential to appreciate it. The world thus becomes part of God's experience and in this way is deeply meaningful to him. [...] Creation satisfied God's eternal disposition to love and to communicate. It reflects an abundant source of self-creativity and intensity of love and delight."[6]

As we can see, Christian theology contains both anthropocentric and biocentric strains. Still, anthropocentrism has dominated for the past 2000 years, resulting in many devoted Christians not caring about the welfare of animals, the mass extinction of species, or the climate crisis. The comparative theologian now asks: Can we possibly learn from other religions to give us intellectual resources to overcome Christian anthropocentrism? Michelle Voss Roberts has intensively discussed how Eastern religions can provide such resources. Can such resources be found in Islam, too? We have to be aware that—as there are different schools of thought in Christianity—there are different schools of thought, also different approaches and interpretations of Qur'anic verses in Islam. Indeed, there is a Muslim tradition similar to

---

5. C. Pinnock, Most Moved Mover. A Theology of God's Openness, Carlisle: Paternoster 2001, 125.
6. Ibid.

the Christian concept of *imago dei* where only human beings are seen as appointed by God as *khalīfas*: successors, delegates, or representatives (see Q 2:30). Of course, a proper interpretation of the Book of Genesis (1:26-28) reveals humans are not on Earth to exploit nature but to take responsible care of it.[7] But still: Such Muslim theologies may *favor* human exceptionalism, as many Christian theologies do using a similar concept. But likewise, there are disputes about a proper interpretation of what the responsibilities of a *khalīfa* are. It is commonly agreed that it includes stewardship over non-human creation. The Assisi Declaration on Humanity and Nature includes an interreligious agreement "[t]hat dominion cannot be anything other than a stewardship in symbiosis with all creatures".[8] *Stewardship in symbiosis* seems to be an interpretation that avoids anthropocentrism without giving up human exceptionalism.

In addition to weighing Biblical and Qur'anic arguments, one may argue that anthropocentric theologies fail to adequately address important ethical issues; and what fails to adequately address important ethical issues must be itself inadequate; thus, anthropocentric theologies are inadequate. However, this line of reasoning is too simplified. It is possible to defend human exceptionalism and still address climate change as a crucial and maybe the most critical ethical challenge humanity has ever faced. It is possible to be aware of our connectedness to the whole ecosystem through symbiosis without believing we are simply a part of the ecosystem. Even a mind-body-dualist can be a dedicated environmentalist! It is possible to think of humans as the

---

7. See V. Hamilton, The Book of Genesis. Chapters 1–17, Grand Rapids: Eerdmans 1990, 138: "What is expected of the king is responsible care over that which he rules. Thus, like 'image,' *exercise dominion* reflects royal language. Man is created to rule. But this rule is to be compassionate and not exploitative. Even in the garden of Eden he who would be lord of all must be servant of all."

8. The Assisi Declarations: Messages on Humanity and Nature from Buddhism, Christianity, Hinduism, Islam & Judaism, 1986, http://www.arcworld.org/downloads/THE%20ASSISI%20DECLARATIONS.pdf.

image of God without interpreting this title as a justification for the exploitation of nature or animals, but rather see it, as outlined, as a special responsibility God has given us for our planet.

I do not want to defend human exceptionalism and anthropocentrism here. But I think we still lack strong arguments why an open view of God is better or more adequate in addressing important social and ethical issues of our days. Personally, I prefer an open view of God not for social or political reasons but because it allows for a vivid relationship between God and human beings, allows for genuine free will and love, and because I believe in a God who created human beings in order to learn from them and grow together with them. The latter issue, a learning God, a God who grows in character—a scandal for most Christian and Muslim thinkers—is something I learned from an engagement with certain Jewish traditions.[9]

Although this motivation is anthropocentric at first, it can easily be extended to non-human creation: God might have wanted a vivid relationship with all of his creatures for their own sake, and he might even have a deep aesthetic appreciation for non-living nature. And as human beings can learn and grow by watching, engaging with, and taking care of nature, God might be able to learn and grow with creation, for example, by showing compassion for suffering animals, even before humans entered into the picture..[10] In light of this, one can hope for a cosmic salvation, which includes not only human beings but all entities being in what Keller calls "cosmic attunement"—an ideal that humans as co-creators can help gradually become a reality.

---

9. See E. Klaphek, Das religiös-säkulare Spannungsfeld des Judentums, in *Säkulares Judentum aus religiöser Quelle*, ed. E. Klaphek & R. Calderon, Berlin: Hentrich & Hentrich 2015, 9-48, 17.

10. A theory of a God who grows in character in relation to creation is defended by Peter Forrest, see *Developmental Theism: From Pure Will to Unbound Love*, Oxford: Clarendon Press 2007.

IQBAL'S PROCESS RELATIONAL WORLDVIEW:
An Islamic Response to Modern Challenges

SAIDA MIRSADRI, Research Associate at the University of Bonn.

Process thought is already known in the Muslim intellectual world; however, it remains part of the Western speculative tradition and is not well received by Muslim thinkers. The reason might lie in the fact that the process model of God is far too antithetical to the classical divine image in monotheistic religions and, all the more, in Islam. Christian process theology has been criticized by Muslim thinkers for, according to them, the process thought ignores the major divine attributes of perfection (by attributing process and change to God) and absoluteness (namely omnipotence and omniscience).[1] However, I am convinced, this needs to be changed.

I strongly agree with Adis Duderija in that "our concept of God has important implications—not only for what kind of abstract theological beliefs we might hold, but also what kind of ethical values we should abide by. And these ethical values form the very backbone of the kind of societal and political norms and ideals we consider normative for human life."[2] He then argues that progressive Islam, realizing

---

[1]. Cf. Nasiri, Mansour, "Divine Immutability: Perfection or Flaw?", *European Journal of Science and Theology* (June 2019, Vol.15, No.3, pp. 1-18).
[2]. Duderija, 59.

this, subscribes to "a panentheistic concept of the Divine and a form of Islamic open-relational/process theology."[3] In saying this, Duderija openly and expressively suggests the significance of an open-relational and process thought.

Quoting Whitehead, Jared Morningstar highlighted the importance of novelty, "so that the massiveness of order does not degenerate into mere repetition," for "these forms of repetition foreclose the possibility of new modes of thinking and being"[4]—with which, I would argue, the Islamic thought is plagued and for which reason, it needs novelty. However, as Morningstar duly mentioned, this novelty of modernity must be "reflected upon the background of a system," which is what would allow for genuine discernment in deciding how to incorporate this material."[5]

I agree with him that the process-relational approach can potentially avoid the pitfalls of repetition while also incorporating the important insights from the three camps of puritanical reformists, traditionalists, and modernists.

However, these two Muslim colleagues did not illustrate what an "Islamic process theology" could and would be like in a practical sense. Or what this "novelty against the background of a system" might look like. Therefore, I would like to demonstrate how this "concept" of Islamic process theology could concretely look. For this purpose, in what follows, I introduce the philosophical system of a Muslim thinker with a process- relational approach to metaphysics and philosophy by the name of Muhammad Iqbal (1877-1938).

Iqbal is a Muslim thinker who, by being well-versed in the Qur'an and Western philosophical thought, can provide the foundation for a novel Islamic philosophical-theological system. As a towering

---

3. Duderija, 62.
4. Morningstar, 35.
5. Morningstar, 36.

intellectual figure in modern South Asian history, Iqbal continues to be revered by many for his poetry, philosophical writings, and contribution to the modernization of Islamic thought. Hasan Azad describes him as "perhaps the greatest of all Islamic modernists, not least because his level of mastery of Western philosophy, in addition to his deep familiarity with the Islamic tradition, was unparalleled by other great Islamic modernists such as Syed Ahmed Khan (1817-1898), Jamal al-Din Afghani (1838-1897), Muhammad 'Abduh (1849-1905) and Syed Ameer Ali (1849-1928)."[6] His great familiarity with the western thought is due to the fact that he obtained his PhD in Europe (1905-1908), where he got to know about ideas of the German Idealists, Whitehead, Bergson, etc. among others.

Iqbal's novel process-relational worldview becomes all the more important when one observes that classical Islamic metaphysics fails to function well in the face of today's serious challenges. Some Muslim thinkers have been trying to engage with these questions and contribute to these discussions; however, the interest in and the attempt to develop new Islamic metaphysical systems—the necessary first step—is meager, if not nonexistent. Given that Muslim speculative tradition bases its arguments on a classical worldview, it fails to properly and coherently address today's questions. So long as Muslim thinkers are content with the classical metaphysics, which is, in its very nature, hierarchical, static, and androcentric – they fail to respond satisfactorily to today's live questions of human rights, women's rights, and ecological crisis, among others.

Inspired by process thought, Christian eco-theologians in recent decades, including Sallie McFague (1933-2019) and Catherine Keller (1953-), have pointed their critiques at the metaphysical hierarchies of classical theism. According to these thinkers, "[t]he idea of

---

6. Hasan Azad, "Reconstructing the Muslim Self: Muhammad Iqbal, *Khudi*, and the Modern Self" in *Islamophobia Studies* (Vol. 2, No. 2, 2014, pp. 14-28), 15.

a transcendent God, lying beyond the created world, motivates this understanding, for traditional cosmological mappings place God at the top of a metaphysical ladder that descends to the human male as God's primary 'image,' then down to the human female, animals, plants, and, finally, inanimate matter."[7] They have rightly criticized this model, "for its justification of human (not to mention male) domination of the earth."[8] Even much less "attention has been paid to the way this hierarchical model also functions to bind humans and non-humans into 'essentialized' roles or identity constructs that limit the modes of relationship possible between them."[9] These theologians also highlight the danger of certain classical divine attributes (i.e., omnipotence and omniscience) that valorize absolute power and domination in an age of alarming ecological and nuclear threats.

I agree with these thinkers, and speaking from the Islamic tradition, I argue that I can find due relevance to the issues and challenges of today's world and responses to them in Muhammad Iqbal's thought. For one, because Iqbal's ontological system encourages a process-relational worldview, in which "consciousness," "creativity," and "life" take center stage, rather than "God" (an abstract theo-centrism and thus the charge of ontotheology) or "man" (androcentrism). Starting his metaphysics from the inner experience of the "human subject" of his/her "being in the world," Iqbal's philosophy assumes that reality is ultimately expressible in terms of a conscious "ego."

Furthermore, Iqbal's robust anthropology places the responsibility for the world's future on humanity. This both encourages us to find ways humans might be more considerate of others and their

---

[7]. Luke Higgins, "Toward a Deleuze-Guattarian Micropneumatology of Spirit-Dust" in *Ecospirit: Religion, Philosophy, and the Earth*, ed. Laurel Kearns and Catherine Keller (New York: Fordham University Press, 2007), 252.
[8]. Ibid.
[9]. Ibid.

environment and discourages us from accepting escapism or fatalism. Therefore, I firmly believe that Iqbal's "neo-classical" metaphysics is more helpful and relevant to today's world and logically more tenable in addressing and responding to many of our philosophical-theological questions.

In what follows, I give a brief introduction to his metaphysics, starting with the key concept of *"khudī."* In a subsequent step, I will demonstrate how this new metaphysics could have alternative implications in our understanding of reality, God, humanity, and a God-world relationship.

Iqbals Metaphysics: The Key Concept Ego/Khudī/Self

The kernel of Iqbal's philosophical-theological system is the concept of *"khudī"*—the Persian term coined by him, and used in his Urdu and Persian poesy, translated as "ego" or "egohood" in his prose. This is the key word in understanding Iqbal's worldview; every other part of his metaphysics revolves around this concept. Iqbal, much like Descartes and German Idealists who came after him, builds his philosophical system upon the ontological understanding of the notion of the "self." He begins his metaphysics by turning his gaze inwards, starting from the human inner conscious experience (i.e., introspection). His starting point is, therefore, our conscious understanding of our being in the world.

Starting from the concept and inner experience of the "self/ego," he moves to the world outside and attributes "egohood" to the whole reality. As in the Cartesian and German idealist tradition, he moves inside-out, from the "subjective experience" to the "objective experience" of the phenomenal world, and not the other way around—which was the approach of classical theism (i.e., from cosmology to epistemology or from the world outside to the human inside). According to Iqbal, and starting with his inner experience of the "self/ego," the whole reality is "egohood:" "All life is individual; there is no such thing as universal life."[10] Thus according to him, "egohood" is the very substance of the whole universe, "[t]hroughout the entire gamut of being runs the gradually rising note of 'egohood,'"[11] which is linked with the idea that there is a will which is free and creative both in us and in the universe. We are conscious of this in our own self, in nature before us, and in the ultimate principle of all life, the Ultimate Ego/God. Therefore, starting with the individual ego as a center of will and energy, Iqbal develops his philosophy, his conception of God, the individual's freedom and will, and human-Nature-God relation.[12] Iqbal's philosophy of *khudī* is "ultimately the foundation of his concept of God."[13]

To formulate it in prepositions his argument would be as follows:

(1) The reality—including "me"—is one (monistic presumption).
(2) Through my first-hand inner experience—untainted by the "filters" of my sense perception and the "categories" of my mind—I perceive (or to use the Whiteheadian term "prehend") a "self."

Being a monist (i.e., an adherent of a philosophical system that emphasizes the oneness or unity of the reality), I can attribute this "selfhood" to the whole reality.

To put it differently, referring to his inner experience and discovering a "self/ego" there, being a monist, Iqbal concludes that the whole reality

---

10. Muhammad Iqbal, *The Secrets of the Self (Asrar-i-Khudi): A Philosophical Poem*, tr. Reynold A. Nicholson (Lahore: Sh. Muhammad Ashraf, 1983), xvii.
11. Muhammad Iqbal, *The Reconstruction of Religious Thought in Islam* (Lahore: Iqbal Academy Pakistan, 2011), 57.
12. I write the word "nature" capitalized, as Iqbal does, though he doesn't explain why. One can guess it is his regard of Nature as part of the divine life (i.e., God's character).
13. M. Irfan Iqbal, "Iqbal's Concept of God: The Birth of Theism in the Philosophy of Iqbal" in *Al-Hikmat* (Vol. 19, 1999, pp. 41-52), 43.

is a community of "egos." By claiming this, he excludes any idea of reality being a blind force (Schopenhauer), an absolute will to power (Nietzsche), or a mere life force (Bergson). According to Iqbal, as an ego, reality is all these—will and life force, but not blind and purposeless. Iqbal adds the element of "rationality" to the picture—and thus "directedness"—and as such defines reality in many passages as "rationally directed creative life (or will)."[14]

Iqbal calls the total of these characteristics "ego." It is "the ultimate ground of all experience, a rationally directed creative will which we have found reasons to describe as an ego."[15] And one of "these reasons," according to him, is the "synthetic" character of this "ultimate ground of experience." In other words, since we discover a synthetic function at work in us that makes a synthesis out of all the plurality perceived by the senses—or outer experience—we infer that this "creative will and life" must be rationally directed, and since these elements are the major characteristics of a "self," Iqbal finds himself justified to call it so. And since he is a monist, he projects his inner experience to the whole reality. Therefore, the whole reality, from the smallest particles to God—who is the Absolute Reality, and as such also called the "Absolute Ego"—are "self"s, what Iqbal terms "*khudī*" or "ego" or "egohood." The reality is nothing but divine energy at work, however, not a mere manifestation of it, since the idea of "egohood," which implies a degree of personality and individuality, implies uniqueness and distinctness: "Every atom of Divine energy, however low in the scale of existence, is an ego. But there are degrees in the expression of egohood."[16] Therefore, reality is a "community of egos" of different levels, based on the degree of consciousness, freedom, will, rationality, etc., and the higher the level of egohood, the higher the level of reality.

---

14. Iqbal 2011, 48, 50.
15. Ibid., 50.
16. Ibid., 57.

Besides the basic characteristics of the ego as being a "rationally directed creative life/will," Iqbal detects another essential characteristic in his inner experience, namely constant change, and movement. Therefore, the "ego" he experiences (or "prehends") cannot be "something rigid"; it is in constant change. It constantly "organizes itself in time and is formed and disciplined by its own experience."[17] From all these characteristics, Iqbal infers yet another feature for the ego, namely "act." Thus his real personality, "is not a thing; it is an act. My experience is only a series of acts, mutually referring to one another and held together by the unity of a directive purpose. My whole reality lies in my directive attitude. You cannot perceive me like a thing in space, or a set of experiences in temporal order; you must interpret, understand, and appreciate me in my judgments, in my will-attitudes, aims, and aspirations."[18]

After defining this key concept of "*khudī*" in Iqbal's metaphysics and his understanding of this basic constituent of reality, I now turn to his conception of the world, of God, and of human beings.

Iqbal's Conception of The World

Scattered in his major prose work, *The Reconstruction of Religious Thought in Islam* (1930)[19] we can find the elements of Iqbal's alternative metaphysical view about the nature of reality. In this respect, he constantly invokes not only the Qur'an but also scholars of both physics and metaphysics. "We have seen that Professor Whitehead describes the universe, not as something static, but as a structure of events possessing the character of a continuous creative flow. This quality of nature's passage in time is perhaps the most significant aspect of experience which the Qur'an emphasizes and which ... offers

---

17. Ibid., 85.
18. Ibid., 83.
19. From here onwards referenced as *The Reconstruction*.

the best clue to the ultimate nature of reality. To some of the verses (3: 190-191; 2: 164; 24: 44) bearing on the point I have already drawn your attention."[20]

Occasionally, and not at all systematically, in his *magnum opus*, *The Reconstruction*, Iqbal attributes certain characteristics to the Reality,[21] which I innumerate here:

1. Free creative movement: On the analogy of our conscious experience, Iqbal concedes, "the universe is a free creative movement."[22] Unlike the traditional view that took substance and matter as fundamental and movement as accidental, for Iqbal, it is movement that is integral to "the Reality."
2. Primacy of event/act: Based on the above discussion, then, we are led to the second characteristic of the Reality, namely the primacy of event/ act—vis-à-vis "substance." Turning the traditional (Aristotelian) substance-based view on its head, Iqbal defends an event-based or an act-based ontology, where the constituents of reality are no longer static substances or "things" but dynamic events or acts (or egos).
3. Change and growth (dynamism): Based on such an understanding of reality, the universe would be regarded as an ongoing process of expansion and change, always in flux. Iqbal regards the Qur'an as his source of inspiration in this regard. "The Qur'an opens our eyes to the great fact of change."[23] Moreover, he repeatedly mentions, throughout *The Reconstruction*, that the universe, according to the Qur'an is liable to and capable

---

20. Ibid., 36.
21. I write the word "Reality" capitalized, as Iqbal does, though he does so without explanation.
22. Ibid., 41.
23. Ibid., 12

of "increase,"[24] that it is "a growing universe and not an already completed product which left the hand of its maker ages ago, and is now lying stretched in space as a dead mass of matter to which time does nothing, and consequently is nothing."[25]

4. Becoming: When constant movement and change are integral to a metaphysics of act/event, then, in such a dynamic system, it is no wonder to see that *becoming* gets primacy over *being*. "We *become* by ceasing to *be* what we are"[26] and there is no ending point to this eternal process of becoming, not even upon death, for life is, in fact, nothing but "a passage through a series of deaths."[27]

5. Organic wholeness/interconnectedness/interrelatedness: Reality is a web of interconnected events, none of which can be separated from others nor survive alone. In his objection to the substance/matter-based Aristotelian universe, Iqbal, inspired by the Whiteheadian view, regards Nature as an organism in a progressive evolution. According to him, the whole universe is "understood as a living, ever-growing organism whose growth has no final external limits."[28] Therefore, despite unceasing, constant change and movement going on, it does not end up in chaos, for "there is a system in the continuity of this passage. Its various stages, despite the apparently abrupt changes in our evolution of things, are organically related to one another."[29]

6. Openness: In Iqbal's metaphysics, "*telos*," which in its traditional sense is understood as a pre-determined external purpose, is strongly refused. "The world-process, or the movement

---

24. Ibid., 44; 45; 102.
25. Ibid., 44.
26. Italics added
27. Ibid., 44.
28. Ibid., 45.
29. Ibid., 44.

of the universe in time, is certainly devoid of purpose if by purpose we mean a foreseen end—a far-off fixed destination to which the whole creation moves. To endow the world-process with purpose in this sense is to rob it of its originality and its creative character."[30] However, he understands purpose or *telos* in another light. "Its ends are terminations of a career; they are ends to come and not necessarily premeditated. A time-process cannot be conceived as a line already drawn. It is a line in the drawing—an actualization of open possibilities". However, the world process is not purposeless either. It is purposive in the sense of being selective in character and in that it "brings itself to some sort of a present fulfillment by actively preserving and supplementing the past."[31] Iqbal then argues that nothing could be more "alien to the Qur'anic outlook than the idea that the universe is the temporal working out of a preconceived plan."[32] Therefore, the future should be regarded as "an open *possibility*," says Iqbal, "and not as a *reality*."[33] He further adds that "[t]he future certainly pre-exists in the organic whole of God's creative life, but it pre-exists as an *open possibility*, not as a fixed order of events with definite outlines."[34]

7. Incompleteness: In stark contrast to the classical metaphysical understanding, Iqbal does not regard the universe as a complete, closed, and determined system. "The universe is not a completed act: it is still in the course of formation. There can be no complete truth about the universe, for the universe has not yet become 'whole.'"[35] Rejecting the traditional view of the

---

30. Ibid.
31. Ibid.
32. Ibid.
33. Ibid., 46.
34. Italics added. Ibid 63.
35. Iqbal 1983, xvii.

created world as a perfectly built construct, Iqbal insists, "It is not a block universe, a finished product, immobile and incapable of change."[36] Rather, according to him, we live in an evolving universe towards perfection, which contains a multitude of organisms, each seeking its complete self-revelation and fulfillment.

8. Purposefulness: Although each part of this universe is an ego with a certain level of consciousness and self-determination, and is interconnected and dependent on other self-determined parts, this does not entail that the universe has an indeterminate nature, with no clear purpose or end. Denying the existence of substance in the universe and granting a level of self-determination to the world does not necessarily mean denying the existence of a *telos*. The whole universe, as a part of the created work of God, is directed toward an end. However, this purpose or end does not mean a pre-determined outline of an externally set destination; it is the inner reach of each finite ego towards infinity (i.e., the Absolute Ego), for there lies its perfection.

These being the characteristics of the reality (ontology) now I turn to Iqbal's understanding of human being (anthropology).

Iqbal's Conception of Human Being

Iqbal believes that egohood, which he attributed to the whole Reality, finds its culmination in mankind. "Throughout the entire gamut of being runs the gradually rising note of Egohood until it reaches its perfection in man [sic]. That is why the Qur'an declares the Ultimate Ego to be '*nearer to man [sic] than his own neck-vein.*'"[37] Human, being the only fully conscious ego in whom egohood finds its perfection, is

---

36. Iqbal 2011, 8.
37. Qur'an 50: 16. Iqbal 2011, 57

God's co-helper in this universal striving for perfection, in this process of becoming and growth. "We are gradually traveling from chaos to cosmos and are helpers in this achievement."[38] Since the universe has not yet become whole and is far from being a complete construction, there cannot be any ultimate truth about it. It is, thus, "human"—as God's *khalifa*/viceroy[39]—who has to do his/her share in this evolutionary, processive project, to help bring form and order into this "chaos," helping to build a "cosmos" out of it.

Since the degree of reality attributed to someone or something correlates with the degree of "I-amness," consciousness, or "egohood" in him/her/it, then human being stands on the highest level in the gradation of the Reality. "Man [*sic*], therefore, in whom egohood has reached its relative perfection, occupies a genuine place in the heart of Divine creative energy, and thus possesses a much higher degree of reality than things around him. Of all the creations of God, he [*sic*] alone is capable of consciously participating in the creative life of his [*sic*] Maker." And s/he alone is to help the world towards betterment. "Endowed with the power to imagine a better world, and to mold what is into what ought to be, the ego in him [*sic*], aspires, in the interests of an increasingly unique and comprehensive individuality, to exploit all the various environments on which he [*sic*] may be called upon to operate during the course of an endless career."[40]

Due to such capacities in him/her, s/he alone is in the position of sharing in the aspiration of the universe and, along with shaping his/her destiny, of guiding the world-process: "It is the lot of man [*sic*] to share in the deeper aspirations of the universe around him [*sic*] and to shape his [*sic*] own destiny as well as that of the universe, now by adjusting himself [*sic*] to its forces, now by putting the whole of his [*sic*]

---

38. Iqbal 1983, xvii.
39. An allusion to the Qur'an (2:30) where God announces to the angels that S/He is going to set a viceroy on the earth.
40. Iqbal 2011, 58.

energy to mold its forces to his [sic] own ends and purposes." And it is in this process of progressive change that "God becomes a co-worker with him [sic], provided man [sic] takes the initiative."[41] Here, he turns his previous formulation on its head and takes a huge step in regarding God as the co-worker to humans rather than the other way around. And this testifies to a the existence of a very robust anthropology in Iqbal's metaphysics.

Iqbal's Conception of God

After having depicted the Iqbalian universe and once detected human's place in it, we can now turn to the concept of God in Iqbal's metaphysics. We'll see what place God occupies in this system and how the divine relates to and acts in the world. Based on Iqbal's pan-psychic view, the whole universe, from the smallest elements to humankind, is a community of egos, with varying degrees of consciousness, freedom, and will in the process of perfection. At the summit of this ontological system stands the Absolute Ego, the telos of creation, towards which all the egos are moving.

The major function God plays in Iqbal's metaphysics in that of order giver.[42] On the one hand, as the Absolute Ego, with the capacity of synthesis, S/He guarantees an organic unity out of the countless (mostly incongruent) pluralities. In other words, God or the Absolute/Ultimate Ego is "an organizing principle of unity" that, through "synthetic activity,"[43] can make syntheses out of the whole range of pluralities. There is no doubt that the organic growth of the Reality, as the unceasing rush of the life force, is in need of a progressive synthesis of its various stages. God is this synthesizing element at work at the heart

---

41. Qur'an 13: 11. Iqbal 2011, 10.
42. This classification and such an attribution to the role and function of God in Iqbal's system is mine, extracted from Iqbal's own views. He himself, however, does nowhere explicitly state anything in this regard.
43. Ibid., 48.

of the Reality. This is reminiscent of the Whiteheadian conception of God as "the principle of limitation" as well as "the provider of structure for the process of events."[44]

On the other hand, God preserves permanence in a world of never-ceasing movement and change. In other words, since the universe is an ongoing process of expansion and change, always in flux, there must be an element of permanence behind all things changing, otherwise it would end up in pure chaos. God is this very element of permanence at work at the heart of the Reality. This Iqbalian idea is also reminiscent of Whitehead, where he states, "[t]he art of progress is to preserve order amid change and to preserve change amid order."[45] Iqbal sees a dialectic between "permanence"—in the Whiteheadian terminology "order"—and "change" at work in the world, which is also constitutive of it.

Divine Attributes

Based on this new metaphysical framework, certain divine attributes get prominence—which traditionally were ignored—and certain traditional interpretations of some other attributes get redefined. Due to the centrality of "egohood" in Iqbal's metaphysics, in defining the divine anew (as the Absolute Ego), he comes up with a different set of attributes for God—which he regards as "the Qur'anic conception of God."[46] These are the following:

1. **Creativity/ Creativeness:** As Iqbal's universe is dynamic and changing, so is his God. The Ultimate Ego is essentially and constantly creative. This is not a mere "contriver" working on something given. According to Iqbal, "God, the Ultimate Ego," is not the classical

---

44. Daniel A. Dombrowski, *A History of the Concept of God: A Process Approach* (New York: SUNY Press, 2016), 216.
45. Whitehead 1978, 339
46. Iqbal 2011, 51.

philosophers' and theologians' static, changeless, transcendent being but a principle of infinite creativity, change and movement. "The 'not-yet' of man [sic] does mean pursuit and may mean failure; the 'not-yet' of God means unfailing realization of the infinite creative possibilities of His [sic] being which retains its wholeness throughout the entire process."[47]

However, this would not at all imply any imperfection on the side of the divine, when concepts like "change" and "perfection" would not be understood within the Aristotelian metaphysics and terminology (what the Muslim thinkers for centuries did): "To the Creative Self change cannot mean imperfection," for the "perfection of the Creative Self consists, not in a mechanistically conceived immobility, as Aristotle might have led Ibn Hazm to think. It consists in the vaster basis of His creative activity and the infinite scope of His creative vision. God's life is self-revelation, not the pursuit of an ideal to be reached."[48]

2. **Knowledge:** Iqbal refrains from using the classical divine attribute of "omniscience" for divine knowledge—despite using the other classical attribute of absoluteness, namely "omnipotence." Moreover, he rejects the traditional understanding of divine knowledge as "passive omniscience" based on his dynamic understanding of the Reality. He defines it as follows: "The alternative concept of divine knowledge is omniscience in the sense of a single individual act of perception which makes God immediately aware of the entire sweep of history, regarded as an order of specific events, in an enteral 'now.'"[49]

Recognizing "an element of truth" in that, he still refutes it since he is strongly convinced that such a conception "suggests a closed universe, a fixed futurity, a predetermined, unalterable order of specific

---

47. Ibid., 48.
48. Ibid.
49. Ibid., 62.

events which, like a superior fate, has once for all determined the directions of God's creative activity."[50] But divine knowledge regarded as such, according to him, is nothing more than the inert void of pre-Einsteinian physics, which confers a semblance of unity on things by holding them together, a sort of mirror passively reflecting the details of an already finished structure of things which the finite consciousness reflects in fragments only."[51] He adds, "If history is regarded merely as a gradually revealed photo of a predetermined order of events, then there is no room in it for novelty and initiation."[52]

Consequently, we can no longer talk of "creation", for this concept can have "a meaning for us only in view of our own capacity for original action."[53] He assumes, thus, that "the whole theological controversy relating to predestination is due to pure speculation with no eye on the spontaneity of life, which is a fact of actual experience."[54] Therefore, Iqbal is, as already mentioned, one of the proponents of the idea of the "open future"—and in that ahead of his time—for he overtly states: "The future certainly pre-exists in the organic whole of God's creative life, but it pre-exits as an open possibility, not as a fixed order of events with definite outlines."[55] That is to say, along with rejecting the existence of any pre-determined end for the world, Iqbal rejects the idea that God can have any real pre-knowledge of the future in its complete actuality. God does not fully know what the result of any specific event will be in its totality until it unfolds itself by time and thus forms the future. God's knowledge about the world is increased by the movement and unfolding of the universe. This does not entail any limitation to divine knowledge, for this "not being able" comes from logical impossibility and not

---

50. Ibid., 63.
51. Ibid.
52. Ibid.
53. Ibid.
54. Ibid.
55. Ibid.

from the restrictions in the divine power. In other words, contrary to what the classical view holds, subscription to the "open future" idea does not necessarily signify God's defective omniscience; it only means, according to Iqbal, that there is yet no future knowledge to be known because the future events are possibilities rather than actualities—and God can only have knowledge of the latter.

Far from accepting the critique of the traditional party in ascribing limitation to his conception of divine knowledge, Iqbal regards their concept of "omniscience" as too narrow and restrictive a concept to be able to do justice to the divine knowledge, for if the divine will were to be understood as dependent on and bound to an order of specific pre-determined events, then such a notion would be opposed to God's living and continuous creative activity, and would as well undermine human free will, as well as the freedom of the created world. Whereas if we are to do justice to God, as the source of life and freedom, then divine knowledge "must be conceived as a living creative activity to which the objects that appear to exist in their own right are organically related. By conceiving God's knowledge as a kind of reflecting mirror, we no doubt save His [sic] foreknowledge of future events; but it is obvious that we do so at the expense of His [sic] freedom."[56] So, according to Iqbal, the classical concept of divine omniscience seeks to guarantee divine foreknowledge at the high price of divesting God of freedom. Based on this understanding, then, the traditional Muslim thinkers defended a conception of divine perfect knowledge that worked *only* at the very high price of depriving both God and humans, as well as the whole created world, of their freedom.

3. **Omnipotence:** Iqbal keeps this traditional divine attribute of absoluteness as one of the major elements of his "Qur'anic conception of God," but still modifies its meaning since he believes omnipotence,

---

56. Ibid.

"abstractly conceived, is merely a blind capricious power without limits."[57] And, thus, tries to give a fresh definition to it. Iqbal views divine omnipotence as intimately related to divine wisdom. At the same time, he argues, the Qur'an conceives God as "holding all goodness in His [sic] hands."[58]

Therefore, God's power is restricted by divine wisdom and goodness. Understood as such, although Iqbal regards omnipotence as one of the divine attributes, his interpretation differs significantly from the orthodox, traditional understanding. According to the conventional conception, God is the ultimate controlling power—he controls every single detail and fiber of the world's causal process. In Iqbal's system of thought, God is also conceived as having absolute power, yet still limited in some respect; thus, not "absolute" in the traditional sense.

God-World Relationship

Now that the place and role of God have become clear in Iqbal's metaphysics, the question would be how to conceive the God-world relationship. Iqbal is strongly against the Greek-inspired Muslim conception of the divine, which rendered the living God of the prophetic religions into an immoveable *causa prima*, for he believes imagining God as the first uncaused cause of the chain of causes can lead, among other things, directly to spreading "fatalism." "Philosophy, searching for the meaning of cause as applied to God, and taking time as the essence of the relation between cause and effect, could not but reach the notion of a transcendent God, prior to the universe, and operating upon it from without. God was thus conceived as the last link in the chain of causation, and, consequently, the real author of all that happens in the universe."[59]

---

57. Ibid., 64.
58. Qur'an 3: 26 and 73; 57:29. Iqbal 2011, 64.
59. Ibid., 88.

Therefore, pure reason that begins with sense experience and ends with speculation leads us astray in understanding the God-world relationship, for it reduces God into a mere concept. This gives us the image of a fully transcendent God, detached from the world, beyond time and space, yet operating on it from without; thus, a kind of deism, or at best, a natural theology. Therefore, the only way open to us is through our inner, direct conscious experience, where we find through and through life force. However, here again, if we rely on the capacity of pure reason in analyzing our inner experience, the result would not be any less flawed, for, according to Iqbal, "[t]he operation of thought which is essentially symbolic in character veils the true nature of life, and can picture it only as a kind of universal current flowing through all things." The result of such a view (i.e., intellectual view of life), therefore, "is necessarily pantheistic."[60]

Therefore, Iqbal's alternative is to imagine God as the Ultimate Ego (to avoid pantheism) as both immanent and transcendent (to avoid deism and absolute transcendence). Although he puts more emphasis on the transcendence of God, according to Enver, neither transcendence nor immanence is exclusively true of his God.[61] Saying God is immanent is another way to highlight the notion that the Realty is God's *creative self-expression*. The physical world is the divine will revealing the infinite creativity and riches of His/Her being. God is immanent, for S/He comprehends and encompasses the whole universe, but also transcendent since S/He is not identical with the created world.

In an attempt to build up his novel metaphysical system, Iqbal tries "to unite in one motion the Absolute of cosmology with the Person of monotheism".[62] His God is neither the detached deity of

---
60. Ibid., 48.
61. Ishrat Hasan Enver, *The Metaphysics of Iqbal* (Lahore: Sh. Muhammad Ashraf, 1944), 75.
62. Whittemore, Robert C., "Iqbal's Panentheism," *in The Review of Metaphysics* (Vol. 9, No. 4, 1956, pp. 681-699), 694.

philosophers nor the impersonal immanent God of Sufi pantheism, who renders everything in the world into mere manifestations devoid of authenticity and reality. His God is the Qur'anic God; the personified Absolute. "Iqbal has sought to accomplish not merely the personalization of the Absolute, but to do so in such a manner as to render his conception true in character and spirit to the teaching of the Qur'an".[63] Since, according to him, Islamic thought has long been dominated by dogmatic scholasticism, which is the heritage of the Greek speculative tradition, Iqbal makes it his task to rid Islam and the Islamic thought of all the Hellenistic and scholastic elements and such reach the heart of the teachings of the Qur'an.

As Whittemore duly states: "Hence, for Iqbal, as for many philosophers and theologians of the West, any revivification of religion must begin with the recognition that the scholastic outlook, far from constituting a divinely sanctioned truth, is rather a philosophical and theological straitjacket of which religion must be divested if it is to live. Applied to Islam, this means a panentheistic reinterpretation of the teaching of the Qur'an, and throughout his work, Iqbal is concerned to show that this teaching is not simply harmonious with his 'reconstruction' but actually requires it."[64]

To regard God as both immanent and transcendent is to understand the God-world relationship in panentheistic terms, and this is Iqbal's conception. God is immanent in and in direct contact with the world. However, "we must not forget that the words proximity, contact, and mutual separation which apply to material bodies do not apply to God." Similar to some Sufis, Iqbal understands the relationship between God and the world "on the analogy of the soul's contact with the body." Just like the "soul is neither inside nor outside the

---

63. Ibid., 694-95.
64. Ibid.

body; neither proximate to nor separate from it," so is God in the world without being identical with the world.[65]

Moreover, Iqbal regards Nature as divine character. His argument here again revolves around his concept of "ego/self." Since "a self is unthinkable without a character (i.e., a uniform mode of behavior)," so is Nature—which "is not a mass of pure materiality occupying a void," but rather "a structure of events, a systematic mode of behavior, and as such organic to the Ultimate Self. Nature is to the Divine Self as character is to the human self."[66] Therefore, God, as the Absolute Ego/Self, must, by definition and logical necessity, have some character. Nature is that divine character.

Conclusion

One can read in Iqbal's body of work the major conviction that the classical understanding of God as the unchanging and unmoving *causa prima*, who sits above and beyond the created world and unaffected and unrelated to it, does not only do injustice to the creator God of Scripture, who is in close relation with the created world—and, as such, fetters the divine freedom—but also leads to a closed and deterministic ontology, that, as a result, also shackles the freedom of human. Not just that, it also leads to some logical-philosophical conundrums, including the problem of evil, the relation between creation and time, the compatibility between divine infallible foreknowledge and human free will, the difficulty of the relation with and the intervention of the supernatural being in the natural world, etc. Detecting the problem as such, Iqbal seeks in his "reconstruction project" to come up with an alternative metaphysics that does away with these difficulties.

There emerges a possibility in Iqbal's metaphysics to seize an alternative conceptualization of a *creator God* who seeks to promote rather

---
65. Iqbal 2011, 108.
66. Ibid., 45.

than undermine the agency, freedom, and self-determination of the created world. Iqbal's novel understanding of omniscience does justice to the elements of spontaneity and novelty inherent in the make-up of finite egos and thus upholds and guarantees freedom in the world, for if the future events were pre-determined at a higher cosmic level by God, then novelty, creativity, human freedom, and spontaneity would be oxymoron.

Iqbal is, of course, well aware of the consequences of his view, the major one being that "the emergence of egos endowed with the power of spontaneous and hence unforeseeable action is, in a sense, a limitation on the freedom of the all-inclusive Ego." However, he regards this limitation unproblematic for his conception of the divine since it is not a limitation "externally imposed" on God, but rather "born out of His [sic] own creative freedom whereby He [sic] has chosen finite egos to be participators of His [sic] life, power, and freedom."[67]

In Iqbal's process, relational worldview, humans (regardless of sex and gender) and Nature (including all its parts, no matter how trivial on the chain of existence) are one and united. Since all are conceived as "egos," the whole world is a "cosmic community" whose members—from the sub-atomic particles to God—are self-determined egos (and thus creative), however, with graded levels of consciousness and freedom. But these individual egos are not fully self-sufficient and independent from one another, since as a *community* (of egos), despite being individuals, they are very closely interrelated. God in this cosmic community is the Absolute Ego, the source of life and creativity, towards whom all creatures strive.

This brings all forms of life—from humans to the subatomic particles—to the same level, transforming the classical anthropocentric and hierarchical worldview into a rather leveled and life-centered worldview. On the other hand, by replacing the classical masculine

---

67. Ibid., 64.

divine attributes of absoluteness (including the highly problematic attributes of omniscience and omnipotence) with the feminine attributes of creativity, life, and relationality, it results in a not just rather feminine worldview but also a more feminine divine image. This way, it can be corrective and complementary to the classical "androcentric" metaphysics (as well as theology), by suggesting a rather feminine and "biocentric" alternative metaphysics.

We should mention that in the face of the imminent threat of environmental and ecological depletion, we are today, more than any time before, aware of the importance of human responsibility and their respectful approach to Nature. Iqbal's life-centric metaphysics helps us bring sanctity back to Nature, which has been desacralized by the modern worldview. It also provides us with a robust anthropology in order to emphasize human responsibility for the future of the world, to which s/he is (as a member of this "cosmic community") is closely interrelated. This is unlike the infantilism and escapism inherent in the classical view, encouraged by its deterministic and closed metaphysics.

We are well-aware now that today, more than any time before, it is of utmost importance to create systems of thought, both philosophical and theological, that are more ecologically sensitive. Additionally, it is imperative that these systems be predicated upon the interdependence of all life forms. Iqbal's metaphysics is one of such systems, and is as such the most befitting example for and the best representative of an Islamic open, relational and process theology/philosophy. And here lies the importance and relevance of his thought to our time.

Bibliography

- Azad, Hasan. "Reconstructing the Muslim Self: Muhammad Iqbal, *Khudi*, and the Modern Self" in *Islamophobia Studies*, Vol. 2, No. 2, 2014, pp. 14-28.
- Dombrowski, Daniel A. *A History of the Concept of God: A Process Approach*. New York: SUNY Press, 2016.

- Enver, Ishrat Hasan. *The Metaphysics of Iqbal.* Lahore: Sh. Muhammad Ashraf, 1944.
- Higgins, Luke. "Toward a Deleuze-Guattarian Micropneumatology of Spirit-Dust", in *Ecospirit: Religion, Philosophy, and the Earth,* edited by Laurel Kearns and Catherine Keller. New York: Fordham University Press, 2007.
- Iqbal, Muhammad. *The Reconstruction of Religious Thought in Islam.* Lahore: Iqbal Academy Pakistan, 2011.
- —————. *The Secrets of the Self (Asrar-i-Khudi): A Philosophical Poem.* Translated *by Reynold A. Nicholson. Lahore: Sh. Muhammad Ashraf,* 1983.
- Iqbal, M. Irfan. "Iqbal's Concept of God; The Birth of Theism in the Philosophy of Iqbal" in *Al-Hikmat*, Vol. 19, 1999, pp. 41-52.
- Nasiri, Mansour. "Divine Immutability: Perfection or Flaw?" in *European Journal of Science and Theology,* Vol.15, No.3, 2019, pp. 1-18.
- Whitehead, Alfred North. *Process and Reality; An Essay in Cosmology.* Corrected edition by David Ray Griffin & Donald W. Sherburne. New York: The Free Press, 1978.
- Whittemore, Robert C. "Iqbal's Panentheism" in *The Review of Metaphysics,* Vol. 9, No. 4, 1956, pp. 681-699.

UNFORESEEABLE POSSIBILITIES:
In Conversation with Saida Mirsadri

MICHAEL LODAHL, Ph.D., Professor of Theology & World Religions Point Loma Nazarene University.

The task before the modern Muslim is ... immense. He has to rethink the whole system of Islam without completely breaking with the past.
—Muhammad Iqbal

There can be no debate regarding the immense importance of Iqbal's 1934 work, *The Reconstruction of Religious Thought in Islam*. To work through this text is to work through a modern classic in speculative philosophy and exhilaratingly adventurous theology. This was, and remains, a bold venture of Islamic thought creatively engaging an increasingly processive, post-Darwinian world. Any and all attempts on the part of Islamic thinkers (and others!) to reappropriate Iqbal now, a century later, should be applauded. It is my delight, then, to offer a companion piece to Saida Mirsadri's fine essay on Iqbal as she highlights the themes that place him genuinely within the conversation that is process-relational theology.

But, of course, the century that separates us from Iqbal must also be taken seriously. If Iqbal wanted to offer a robust and dynamic interpretation of Islam that could address the problems of modernity—including, to be sure, the fading gasps of Western colonialism—then we must acknowledge our postmodern, post-colonial, ecologically threatened situation. "Modern man" has taken us to the very edge of the erasure of the human species, along with a vast number of other species within God's good creation. That, of course, is not Iqbal's fault! But it means we must read him—especially those of us who collectively have personally benefitted from the modernist vision—with a grain of salt.

Mirsadri points out that Iqbal proposed a strong anthropology. Given his desire to energize and embolden his fellow Muslims in the face of oppressive Western colonialism, this is eminently understandable. But one may suspect that he too freely borrowed the ideological weapons of Western modernism. On the very first page of *Reconstruction* he insists that "Religion, in its more advanced forms, ... in its attitude towards the ultimate reality is opposed to the limitations of man; it [religion] enlarges his claims and holds out the prospect of nothing less than a direct vision of Reality."[1] In the era and mood in which we find ourselves, we are not at all likely to think that we have a "direct vision" of *anything*, to say nothing of reality with a capital R. This, I believe, is all to the good. The more we can acknowledge and even celebrate our deep limitations in knowing—that is, the more we recognize that we are always interpreters of our surroundings, of our texts and traditions, of ourselves and of others—the less likely, presumably, we will be to weaponize our ideas (including our religious ideas).

Such considerations place Iqbal in an unusual, interestingly problematic space. Allow me to illustrate this by engaging his interpretation of the biblical and qur'anic story of the human naming the animals (Gen. 2:18-20; Surah 2:30-34).

First, let us recall some of the fascinating details we encounter in the biblical version of the story. Unlike in Genesis 1, where God

---

1. M. Iqbal, *The Reconstruction of Religious Thought in Islam* (New Delhi: Kitab Bhavan, 1974), 1.

consistently sees creation to be good (*tov*) with each day's labor, in Genesis 2, God observes that "it is not good that the *adam* should be alone" (2:`18)—and *so* "out of the ground the LORD God formed [creatures of land and sky] and brought them to the human *to see what he would call them*; and whatever the human called each living creature, that was its name" (2:19). It is particularly striking that God does this "to see what [the *adam*] would call them," the obvious implication being that whatever names the human might propose are not known, ahead of time, to the deity. Further, the text betrays no suggestion that the Maker provided cue cards or even helpful hints along the way. Instead, the text of Genesis announces straightforwardly, "and whatever the human called every living creature, that was its name" (2:19). Indeed, the text goes even further by observing that after naming all of these creatures, "for *ha adam* there was not found a helper for a partner"—as though to suggest that perhaps both the Holy and the human had harbored hopes for a "helper" among the horde of freshly-minted creatures. None has proven capable of providing a partnering reply to the human. Only then is a partner fashioned from the very side of the human.

Particularly when one considers the fundamental importance of the act of naming in Semitic cultures, it is striking that in Genesis 2, this role is left by the Creator to human ingenuity and creativity. Further, human freedom and creativity appear to necessitate an open and unknown future for the world. The text suggests more than a hint of divine curiosity about what the human will do—keep in mind that God brings the various creatures to the human "to see what [*ha adam*] would call them"—and of course, this narrative detail points us toward a radical openness regarding the future. This future is not a fixed collection of events, not even for God. God offers the task of naming the elements of creation to the human, giving *ha adam* the kind of room and freedom to make, and to keep, the human vocation in the world a relatively open vista. In this story, there are no "right" names, no divinely-prescribed meanings for the world and its creatures; we find instead a thoroughly human partnership, collaborating with God's creativity by acts of observation, discovery, naming, and meaning-making.

By stark contrast, the Qur'an proclaims that God "taught Adam the names of all things" (2:31) and did so, it appears, largely as a way to keep the angels in their place after they had questioned the wisdom of God's stated intention to make a *khalifa* or divine representative on earth, i.e., humanity. So after teaching the human the right and proper names of everything (perhaps only the other creatures are implied here, but perhaps even more things!), God turns to the angels and challenges them to "tell the names of these" (2:31). The angels' reply is, I believe, the proper Muslim response as far as the Qur'an is concerned: "Glory to You! We have no knowledge, except what You have taught us. In truth it is You who are perfect in knowledge and wisdom" (2:32). Both the angels and the human are passive recipients of the truth encoded in the "true names" of all things. There is a true, right, and proper name for everything—and only God knows what that name is. Created intellects stand, apparently, in a radically dependent and passive position in relation to these truths in the mind of God.

This is the sort of uphill climb that confronted and challenged Iqbal. In his initial treatment of the Qur'anic story, he writes that "the point of these verses is that man is endowed with the faculty of naming things, that is to say, forming concepts of them, and forming concepts of them is capturing them."[2] Aside from the disconcerting language of "capturing" things that hedges toward an aggressive, even warlike, orientation toward the world[3], one wonders whether Iqbal has stretched the Qur'anic story beyond recognition. If in the Qur'an

---

2. Ibid., 13.
3. Indeed, immediately thereafter Iqbal adds, "Thus the character of man's knowledge is conceptual, and it is with the weapon of this conceptual knowledge that man

God alone *knows* the *right* names for each and every thing, which obviously implies that there *is* a "right name" of each thing and that God (and God alone) *teaches* the human these right names—then can it properly be said that this story is about God endowing humanity "with the faculty of naming things"?

Granted, in his modernist leanings, Iqbal desired to portray—or perhaps truer to his book's title, to reconstruct—Islam as a tradition that validates human conceptual and linguistic capacities. So we see that in his reading of the Adam story in Surah 2, Iqbal affirms and even celebrates human creativity. Indeed, his interpretation seems to veer toward the Genesis version of the story where the Maker brings all these creatures to the human "to see what he would name them," with the strikingly blunt addendum, "and whatever the human called each creature, *that was its name*" (2:19). One might imagine Iqbal admiring the biblical rendition. And yet later in his book Iqbal seems to offer a differing interpretation of the qur'anic story, one less celebratory of the human as world-knower (and world-conqueror): this time, the passage is "describing Adam's superiority over the angels in remembering and reproducing the names of things."[4] To *re*member, to *re*produce, is not to create but to imitate. Of course, I cannot know whether or not Iqbal would have recognized any appreciable difference between his first characterization of the story and his second; it is nonetheless arguable that in this second allusion to this story of humanity's naming of the world, Iqbal gravitates toward the portrait of the human as passive recipient rather than creative actor. This, of course, is not at all the direction that his book takes, but it may be an indication of the tension that he experienced, at some level, as

---

approaches the observable aspect of Reality" (13). A weaponized epistemology paves the way for a suicidal (anti-)ecology.

4. Ibid., 86.

he strove to "rethink the whole system of Islam without completely breaking with the past."[5]

Iqbal was quick to acknowledge the sort of past Islam with which he was determined to break. It would be an Islam of passivity, of entire acquiescence to a future of preprogrammed inevitabilities issuing from the inscrutable will of God. The Islam he offered to his readers is characterized by adventurous co-creativity with God. In other words, it was closer to Genesis 2 than to Surah 2 (if for a moment we can think of these stories apart from their histories of interpretation!). To do this effectively, though, required some apologetics: "But is it not true, you will say, that a most degrading type of fatalism has prevailed in the world of Islam for many centuries? This is true, and has a history behind it … due partly to philosophical thought, partly to political expedience, and partly to the gradually diminishing force of the life-impulse which Islam originally imparted to its followers."[6] Of these elements Iqbal identifies, the one most crucial to his overall tack is the last: that earliest Islam, rooted in Muhammad's ecstatic mystical experiences, bequeathed a "force of the life-impulse" (think Henri Bergson, among other influences) to its followers. This was a shared experience of vitality, creativity, wonder, and divine immediacy. "That is why the Qur'an declares the Ultimate Ego to be nearer to man than his own neck-vein. Like pearls do we live and move and have our being in the perpetual flow of Divine life."[7] If somehow this experience of adventurous wonder had dissipated among Muslims, it was Iqbal's yearning to open up conceptual and religious space for such an experience to be rekindled.

In my reading of Iqbal, there are two especially noteworthy ideas that help to frame that space for Islamic religious and intellectual renewal:

---

5. Ibid., 97.
6. Ibid. 110.
7. Ibid., 72.

1) While Islam has traditionally recognized Muhammad as "the seal of the prophets," i.e., God's final and authoritative messenger for all time and all people until the end of the world, Iqbal offered a creative twist to this traditional conviction. Muhammad, as "the seal of the prophets," has typically been understood to mean that his message, embodied as the Qur'an, is the ultimate revelatory word. Further, this word is a divine recitation from God to the angel Gabriel to Muhammad; like the human being taught the right names for everything, so Muhammad was a passive recipient of the Arabic words of the Qur'an from God. As perfect divine recitation, the Qur'an is the seal of all previous revelatory texts and, correspondingly, Muhammad is the final and ultimate human spokesperson for God. Accordingly, this has traditionally elevated Muhammad's revelatory status.

Iqbal, however, suggested otherwise: "In Islam, prophecy reaches its perfection in discovering the need of its own abolition. This involves the keen perception that life cannot forever be kept in leading strings; that in order to achieve full self-consciousness man must final be thrown back on his own resources."[8] For Iqbal, Muhammad as "the seal of the prophets" signifies the closure, presumably at the time of Muhammad's death, of the prophetic stage in human history; beyond Muhammad, human beings (and presumably Muslims in particular) are being beckoned by God toward a quality of freedom and creativity not typically imagined in Islam. To return to the variant renditions of the story of humanity assigning names to the creatures and components of the world, Iqbal can be understood to be shifting from the Qur'anic version and toward the biblical version in his interpretation of Muhammad as "the

---

8. Ibid., 126.

seal of the prophets." Prophecy instigates its own abolition by discouraging an infantile faith in prophetic deliverances. After Muhammad, Iqbal argued, humanity is called to an adult relationship with God where responsible partnership is the model.

2) This has intriguing implications for the ways in which we might imagine God in relationship to time and to history, a relationship that, in fact, occupies much of Iqbal's creative thinking in *Reconstruction*. If Islam traditionally has often been hamstrung by the notion of history as the coming to fruition of a set of divinely preprogrammed inevitabilities, Iqbal offered a radically different vision of things as a lure to human creativity. It is difficult to imagine the degree of surprise that the following may have created (or still creates) for a great many of his readers: "The world process, or the movement of the universe in time, is certainly devoid of purpose, if by purpose we mean a foreseen end—a far-off fixed destination to which the whole creation moves. To endow the world process with purpose in this sense is to rob it of its originality and its creative character.[9] Indeed, the idea of "a far-off fixed destination to which the whole creation moves" sounds like the sort of eschatology that dominates much of traditional Judaism and Christianity, let alone Islam. But here, Iqbal was adventurously willing to imagine an alternative, far more open-ended eschatology of the sort one might tend to find among process and some open theists: *the future is open*. A variety of possibilities exist, and indeed those possibilities become compounded and complexified with each passing moment. Iqbal continued:

> A time-process cannot be conceived as a line already drawn. It is a line in the drawing—an actualization

---

9. Ibid., 54.

of open possibilities.... To my mind nothing is more alien to the Quranic outlook than the idea that the universe is the temporal working out of a pre-conceived plan.... It is a growing universe and not an already completed product which left the hand of its Maker ages ago, and is now lying stretched in space as a dead mass of matter to which time does nothing, and consequently is nothing.[10]

For Iqbal, the universe is growing, dynamic, pliable, and open-ended. These characteristics also necessitate that the universe is essentially temporal. Time is real and significant. God dwells intimately *with us* creatures of time and place, change and act. In such a vision of things where the future is "a line in the drawing"—and where creatures such as we have a hand in that continual drawing—what we do in the next moment inevitably creates unforeseeable possibilities leaning toward peace, healing, compassion, love ... or otherwise.

---

10. Ibid., 55.

A CALL FOR A UNITED FAITH RESPONSE TO OUR CURRENT CLIMATE CRISIS

GREG BOYD, Ph.D., Senior Pastor, Woodland Hills Church, Maplewood, MN, adjunct professor of Anabaptist Studies, Northern Seminary.

At the advice of a friend several years ago, I began looking into the science behind global warming.[1] It has, quite frankly, been the most sobering experience of my life! I learned, for example, that the Arctic was warming four times faster than the rest of the planet, on average, and that it has lost almost two-thirds of its total ice mass over the last forty years. And I learned that this is wreaking havoc with the earth's climate. Among other things, the all-important Jet Stream is slowing down and wobbling, and this is a primary explanation for the increasingly intense and increasingly frequently extreme weather events we've been witnessing, especially over the last decade.

For over thirty years, Climatologists have been warning us that unless we immediately take drastic measures to reduce our burning of fossil fuels, the frequency and intensity of our floods, droughts, fires, hurricanes, tornadoes, as well as pandemics will, in all probability,

---

[1]. My primary sources of information are *The International Panel on Climate Change* (https://www.ipcc.ch); *Artic News* (http://arctic-news.blogspot.com); T*he Climate Emergency Institute* (https://www.climateemergencyinstitute.com); Michael Mann, *The New Climate Wa*r (Public Affairs, 2021); Richard Heinberg, *Power: Limits and Prospects for Human Surviva*l (New Society Publishers 2021).

continue to accelerate exponentially into the foreseeable future. And while many nations have set goals to reduce their reliance on fossil fuels by such-and-such dates, very few nations have met them. Indeed, we are currently pumping 65 percent more CO2 into our atmosphere than in 1988, the year the IPCC was formed to set guidelines for the global reduction of fossil fuels!

As a result, more and more climatologists concede that global warming is posing "a direct existential threat," and not sometime in the distant future, and not just for humans.[2] We are currently losing 150 to 200 species of animals, fish, and insects every day. Since 1970 the planet's wildlife population has declined by over 50% and by some estimates, our oceans will be free of eatable fish by no later than 2050! There is no consensus as to when this loss of biodiversity and increasing climate chaos might lead to humanity's extinction, but there is broad agreement that our window of opportunity to avert the most disastrous effects of climate change is closing more quickly than anyone previously thought.

Now, many put their hope in humanity's often-demonstrated ability to innovate our way out of life-threatening situations, and there are some promising new climate change-related developments in the works.[3] But I am persuaded by those who argue that, even if we succeed at developing technologies that can be applied to the scale that would be required to begin to slow and eventually reverse global warming, this would only buy us a little more time unless this technology isn't accompanied by a rather drastic change in the way

---

[2]. See https://sdg.iisd.org/news/un-secretary-general-urges-leadership-to-face-direct-existential-threat-of-climate-change/.

[3]. For a review of new technologies to fight global warming, see *Just Have a Think*, (https://www.youtube.com/c/JustHaveaThink).

we humans tend to envision our relationship to the earth and animal kingdom.[4]

Most importantly, our future survival requires us to abandon the mindset that has gotten us into this climate crisis. For the last two centuries, and especially since the post-WWII "great acceleration," we have adopted an economic model that requires perpetual growth, and hence the perpetual increase of energy, just to sustain itself.[5] Consider that America is currently on pace to double its economy every 22 years. This means that American's consumption of energy must double every 22 years, and currently, 89% of this new energy comes from fossil fuels! This is simply unsustainable, and unless the populations of first-world countries, in particular, do an about-face on a global scale and immediately begin to reduce our consumption and thus our carbon imprint, there is no forthcoming technology that will do anything more than buy us a little more time.

So, while scientists work on climate-saving technologies, the question the rest of us must be considering is how we can hope to change the thinking of the global population, and especially the thinking of those who live in countries that have benefited the most from the use of fossil fuels and have thus contributed the most to the heating up of our planet.

Here is where I believe Jews, Christians, and Muslims have an opportunity to play a vital, prophetic role in our world. For the Qur'an and the traditions of the Prophet Muhammed, as well as the Hebrew Scriptures that Jews and Christians regard as an inspired authority, teach us that this world is created and loved by God and that God has entrusted the well-being of the earth and animal kingdom to

---

4. E,g, Heinberg, *Power*. Helm, *Net Zero*; Tim Jackson, *Post-Growth, Life After Capitalism* (Polity, 2021).
5. J. B. McNeill, Peter Engelke, *The Great Acceleration: An Environmental History of the Anthropocene Since 1945* (Harvard University Press, 2014).

humans.[6] Moreover, our spiritual authorities warn us of the dangers of greed and the blessedness of living simply as well as the dangers of exploiting the earth and animal kingdoms and being apathetic about their own well-being.[7]

For Jews, Christians, and Muslims, taking responsibility for the welfare of the earth and animal kingdom isn't something we should take seriously only because not doing so has brought us to our current "existential threat." Rather, this is simply what being faithful looks like for us. This is what we should have been doing all along. And in light of our current ecological crisis, I can't imagine shared convictions more important than these. It's true that historically speaking, Jews, Christians and Muslims have not been generally known to find a common cause with one another. But if ever there was a cause that we should be able to rally around, *it is this one*. And if ever there was a time to do so, *it is now*.

So, I've recently been wondering and praying about what it might look like for an increasing number of Jews, Christians, and Muslims to raise our collective voice on the urgency of addressing climate change. What might it look like for Jews, Christians, and Muslims to wrestle together with questions of how we can best reverse our current course and begin to pursue simpler, less waste-producing ways of life? What might it look like for people of faith to join the growing movement of people around the globe who are already voluntarily sacrificing modern conveniences when doing so contributes to the well-being of the earth and animal kingdom? What might it look like for people of faith

---

[6]. On the mandate for Muslims to take responsibility for the earth and animal kingdom, see Ibrahim Ozdemir, *Environment and Islam* (https://www.academia.edu/36850188/Environment_and_Islam). For an excellent source on the mandate for Christians and Jews to do so, see https://www.creationjustice.org/mission.html.

[7]. E.g. *Quran* 89:15-25; Luke 12:13-21. See Himmit Surab Pur, *The Perfect Role Model: The Prophet of islam*, (https://www.al-islam.org/perfect-role-model-prophet-islam-himmat-suhrab-pur/living-modestly). Luke 12:13-21.

to provide examples to the rest of the world of how to live sustainable lives?

In fact, I submit that Jews, Christians, and Muslims should be leading this movement precisely because, as I've already mentioned, we are motivated not just by the threat of climate change but by the call of our shared faith. As the catastrophic effects of global warming grow more intense and become more frequent in the years to come, more and more people will be waking up to the existential threat posed by climate change. And hopefully, many of these people will begin to explore ways to reduce their carbon imprint and push back on climate change in any way they can. But I believe that Jews, Christians, and Muslims could, and should, play a leading role in this movement, together.

What might do even more good for our world than our combined voice and efforts combating climate change is the sheer fact that the world would get a chance to witness significant numbers of Jews, Christians, and Muslims working together for an urgent common cause! This would give instant credibility to our voice on climate change and serve as a magnificent beacon of unity and hope to a global population that is feeling increasingly fragmented and hopeless.

Finally, I would contend that Jews, Christians, and Muslims who embrace an Open- Relational understanding of God and of God's intimate relationship with his creation are in the best position to adopt this call. Whereas many of our fellow believers consider everything that comes to pass to be reflective of God's all-determining will, we interpret our sacred scripture and sacred traditions in ways that ascribe significant agency to humans. We understand that God longs to partner with us to see his creation flourish. And we understand that God and his creation are deeply affected by what humans do and do not do. And, perhaps most importantly, we believe that the future is not written in stone but is rather a domain of possible outcomes, which is why we, of all people, should be most passionate about embracing hope for a better future and most passionate about doing all we can do to bring this future about.

I thus believe that it is incumbent on Jews, Christians, and Muslims who share this Open-Relational understanding of God to begin to explore together ways we can better live out our call to care for the earth and animal kingdom and how best to model this for the rest of the world. But we must do so quickly, for our window of opportunity is rapidly closing.

Editor's Note: A response to Greg Boyd by Prof. Dr. Aaron Langenfeld from The Faculty of Theology in Paderborn can be found at https://youtu.be/1aRPX0tXRaI?si=4M8UV-eMnqq0kiTa

THE SOCIAL AND POLITICAL CONSEQUENCES OF OPEN THEOLOGY.
An Islamic perspective

Prof. Dr. MOUHANAD KHORCHIDE, Head of the Center for Islamic Theology at the University of Münster (Germany) and Professor of Islamic Religious Education.

Open Theology shares an important denominator with theology of freedom: both define the God-human relationship as a relationship of freedom. According to this, God has endowed man with freedom so that God intervenes in the world only in a way that does not destroy or impair man's freedom. While God inspires man to expand his horizon, it is up to man himself to make God's will an experienceable reality in the world through his own actions. In other words, God intervenes in the world mainly through man and through his actions. If man fails, then the will of God remains unfulfilled.

Now, one can speculate whether God intentionally makes himself dependent on man or cannot help but make himself dependent on man because he cannot intervene directly in the world. The Islamic tradition has hardly pursued this question since "God's omnipotence" has been understood to mean that God can do anything he wants. If God could not intervene in the world directly, this would deny him his omnipotence. I want to avoid this debate about God to avoid losing myself in metaphysics because everything remains speculative in the end. Also, the Qur'an allows both positions for understanding God's omnipotence because it is ultimately a matter of interpretation.

What I find much more interesting, however, is to ask the question from man's perspective: How free is man to determine his own actions? A direct intervention of God in the world would mean that it is not man who is at work, but God. In my eyes, this is like a declaration of death for man. Because he exists, yet without having the freedom to determine himself, he is only a puppet of creation. To think of man, on the other hand, as a self-determining subject puts the rudder of history back in his hands. It is man who writes and directs his own history. God inspires him in this through his spirit. That means God is not passively watching; he is also at work, but without interfering with man's freedom.

Man, and not God, as the writer and director of history, however, means that man shoulders a great responsibility. The course of history depends on him alone. Whether peace, prosperity, and charity prevail in the world or war, poverty, and suffering, man alone is responsible for it. And it is precisely this idea of an Open Theology that makes religion a crucial source of morality and responsibility for a fulfilled life.

To be religious means to take responsibility for oneself, one's fellows, and the creation, knowing that nothing will change in the world unless man does so. In this regard, the Qur'an says, "God does not change the situation of a people until the people change themselves." (Qur'an 13:11)

However, there is a flip side to this idea: both in history and in the present, there were and are people who legitimized their actions, even violent ones, by claiming that they were acting on God's behalf. They claim that they are merely God's hand, or as some Caliphs called themselves, God's shadow on earth.

However, before I discuss the consequences of Open Theology in Islam, I would like to take a look at some crucial historical developments in order to expose the talk of a God who intervenes directly in the world as a product of political struggles for power.

Already within the first years after the death of the Prophet Muhammad in 632, there existed within the Islamic tradition the first outlines of a later long-lasting theological debate about the question of God's freedom and man's freedom, as well as the relationship of both freedoms to each other. The debate was overshadowed, at first, by the political events surrounding the legitimization of the rule of the Umayyad caliph Mu'awiya (he ruled from 661 to 680)[1], it was nevertheless accompanied from the beginning by a theological reflection, which led to the emergence and later to the establishment of some schools of thought within Islamic theology, which have taken corresponding positions on this question of God's freedom and that of human beings.

Among the most important questions were: Who creates man's actions, God or man? Who is responsible for evil in the world, and why does it exist at all? Which will ultimately prevail, God's will or man's? How free is man really? These questions, and others like them, are important, for they influence each position, one advocating for God's freedom at the expense of human freedom and the other advocating human freedom at the expense of God's freedom. The former position was initially held by the so-called Jabrīya (the determinists) and later by the Ash'arite school.[2] The second position was at first defended by the Qadarīya (representatives of free will) and later it became the position of the Mu'tazilites.[3]

---

1. See Schebli Nu'man in FN 1 p. 50 Mutahhari Qudra.
2. Named after the scholar Abū l-Hasan 'Alī ibn Ismā'īl al-Asch'arī (d. 935).
3. The Mu'tazila is until today the so-called rationalist school of thought in Islam, which had its high point in the history of Islamic ideas in the 8th and 9th centuries. The Abbasid Caliph al-Ma'mun (813-833) declared its teachings to be state doctrine. The school enjoyed the highest ruler's protection in his time and at the time of the Caliphs al-Mu'tasim bi-'llāh (833-842) and al-Wāthiq bi-'llāh (842-847). Several well-known Mu'tazilites were appointed to the Abbasid court during this period, including Abū l-Hudhail and an-Nazzām. The Caliph al-Mutawakkil (847-861) then banned this school, which soon led to its demise.

In these classic debates, it was customary for God's will and freedom to be pitted against man's will and freedom. However, modern conceptions of freedom and theology offer perspectives that allow us to see the discussion as complementary rather than competitive. I will discuss this below and try to show how this way of thinking of freedom is compatible with the Qur'an. It enables us to recast omnipotence as a God-human relationship best understood as a relationship of freedom instead of subjugation.

The political background of the debate about human freedom

The first "school" within the history of Islamic intellectual thought to address the issue of man's free will, emphasizing and defending it, was the so-called qadarite school (al-Qadarīya).[4] This designation is, in fact, not a self-designation but rather a pejorative designation used by the opponents of the al-Qadarīya - and followers of the al-Qadarīya never used it to refer to themselves.[5] The word "Qadarīya" is derived from the Arabic word Qadar (fate) and refers to those who assume that man is in control of his own destiny and thus possesses free will. Scholars such as Ali Sami Annashar or Mutahhari see, in the designation "Qadarīya," an attempt to defame this group and therefore propose the designation "the school of free will" (Arab. *maddhab al-irāda al-ḥurra*).[6] The background of the inner-Islamic debate about the freedom of the human will was, however, first and foremost, a political one.[7]

The issue of human responsibility for one's actions was of great significance as early as the first years of the Umayyad dynasty. On the one hand, the existence of free will was backed up by a powerful

---
4. See Mutahhari al-Insan walqadar (der Mensch und das Schicksal) p. 56.
5. See I of Islam und auch Mutahhari p. 47.
6. See Mutahhari p. 46.
7. See Naschar p. 315.

argument - responsibility, even on judgment day, presupposes freedom. God cannot hold us accountable if our actions are not based on free will. On the other hand, the idea of God being the unique source of all actions and the corresponding concept of determinism played a vital role as early as during the years Muʿāwiya (the first Umayyad Caliph) was in power.

Muʿāwiya referred to both these ideas in a sermon addressed to his soldiers just before the war against the fourth caliph Ali. He used them as explanation for two important events: "And it is part of our fate, determined by God, that he has led us here, and that this is happening between us and the inhabitants of Iraq; because in the Qur'an God says: 'if God had pleased, they would not have fought a war, but God does as He pleases.'" When Muʿāwiya appointed his son Yazīd as his political successor, effectively turning the Caliphate into a monarchy, he said, "The issue with Yazīd is determined by Divine Fate, man has no say in this."[8]

Muʿāwiya was not only the founder of the first Islamic restrictive dominion but also played a vital role in establishing the doctrine of Predestination. When Yazīd succeeded Muʿāwiya after his death, Yazīd said, "Praise be to God, who does as He pleases, and who gives to whom He pleases."[9] He does refer to the Qur'an here, but in order to legitimize his rule and to suggest that it was intended and willed by God. This means that any form of political opposition could thus be condemned as religious opposition to God's will.

With the beginning of the Umayyad dynasty, the doctrine of determination found its way into Islamic theology.[10] Politically, this doctrine was important to validate political rule as the realization of divine will, thus equating any political opposition with an oppositional

---

8. Ibid., 80.
9. Ibid.
10. See Mutahhari p.50 ff.

attitude to God's will.[11] The Qadarīya emerged in the 690s[12] as a reaction to this political instrumentalization of the doctrine of predestination by the Umayyads.

The scholar Maʿbad b. ʿAbd Allāh al-Djuhanī is said to have been the first representative of the Qadarīya.[13] He was a disciple of the well-known companion of the Prophet Abu Tharr, who himself was a professed opponent of the Umayyads.[14] Al-Djuhanī was executed in 703 after the revolt against Ibn al-Ashʿathh.[15]

The Historian of religion Naschar cites several Islamic sources that do not declare Maʿbad al-Djuhanī to be the first representative of human free will, but rather a Christian from Iraq named Wawsan, who converted to Islam but later became a Christian again.[16] However, Nashar sees in it an apologetic that seeks to declare the doctrine of free will as foreign to Islam and to present it as foreign influences from Christianity.[17] Maʿbad al-Djuhanī and his doctrine of free will continued to influence theological discourse even after his death, especially in Iraq and Syria, where it has been widely disseminated.[18] The Turkish historian Taşköprüzade Ahmet (d. 1561) even sees a continuous line between the teachings of Maʿbad al-Djuhanī and Wāṣil ibn ʿAṭāʾ (d. 748), who is considered the founder of the Muʿtazila.[19] The historian al-Maqdesi names one Amr al-Maqsus as the first scholar in Syria to advocate free will explicitly. He was a teacher and advisor to the Umayyad Caliph Muʿāwiya ibn Yazīd (also known as Muʿāwiya the Second, d. 684), who appropriated the doctrine of free will and

---

11. See Yasin p. 133f und Naschar p. 314f.
12. See I of Islam.
13. See Naschar p. 317 und Mutahhari p. 50.
14. Ibid. 317f.
15. See EI.
16. See Naschar p. 319.
17. Ibid.
18. Ibid., 320.
19. See FN 4 und FN 5 bei Nschar p. 320.

was positively taken with it. This attitude of his was no longer compatible for the Caliph with the Caliphate and its claims to power, so he resigned from the Caliphate after a few days.[20] In his farewell speech, he justified his resignation with the injustices committed by his father and grandfather. For their part, the Umayyads accused Amr al-Maqsus of manipulating the resigned caliph and tortured him to death.[21]

A third scholar, Gaylan ibn Muslim, is also considered one of the first scholars to advocate free will. He went to Damascus and had a great influence on their scholars.[22] His discussions with the caliph ʿUmar ibn ʿAbd al-ʿAzīz (717-720) have reached us through various channels,[23] showing his clear position in favor of free will and his corresponding arguments, as well as the arguments of his opponents. The end of Gaylan ibn Muslim was not unlike the two other founders of this school of free will. The Caliph Hishām ibn ʿAbd al-Malik had him tortured and then killed in 723.[24] After his death, the school named after him, al-Gaylaniyya, was formed, which strongly advocated the doctrine of free will. It was political in nature, but its teachings had a great influence in establishing the Muʿtazila.

At this point, it must be emphasized that even if the early discussions on the free will of man were politically motivated, a theological debate on the subject also existed in parallel. The spiritual opponents of the so-called Qadarīya were the Jabrīya, who assumed the determination of man. One of determinism's first and most radical representatives was the scholar Jahm b. Ṣafwān. The historian al-Shahrestānī transmitted the following statement from Ibn Ṣafwān: "Man does not possess the capacity to perform an action. Nor should he be called capable, rather he is determined in his actions, neither does he possess

---

20. Naschar p. 321.
21. Ibid.
22. Naschar p. 321f
23. FN 2 und 3 p. 322.
24. FN 1 p. 324.

ability, nor his own will, nor the ability to choose, rather God creates the actions in him, similar to how God creates this in all non-beings. Actions are attributed to man only in an allegorical sense, similar to the way they are attributed to non-living beings, for example when it is said: 'The tree brings forth fruit'; 'the water flows'; 'the stone moves'; 'the sun rose and set'; [...] also the divine reward and punishment is determined, similarly the actions, they are also determined. And if the determination is certain, then also the responsibility itself is determined."[25] In another statement handed down to us by al-Ashʿarī, he further specifies the difference between man and non-living beings: "God has created man a power through which action becomes possible and He has created for him the will to act and has given only to him the freedom to act."[26] In this he evokes the concept of *kasb* (man's appropriation of the actions created by God) among the Ashʿarites, which ultimately results in a strongly deterministic position.

The scholar al-Ḥasan al-Baṣrī (who died in 724) was one of the first who opposed this concept of determinism in a letter to the Caliph ʿAbd al-Malik Ibn Marwān (who died in 705). He quoted several Qurʾanic verses such as, "Pharaoh thus led his people astray and did not guide them rightly."[27] However, the Umayyads invoked other verses such as, "Whomever God guides is well-guided; and whomever He leads astray – those are the losers."[28]

One of al-Baṣrī's followers, Wāṣil Ibn ʿAṭā (who died in 748), analyzed this issue in more detail. The Muʿtazilite school of thought was founded based on his works, in which he proclaimed that human beings are responsible for their actions and not God, which is why we

---

25. FN 2 Naschar p. 343.
26. FN 5.
27. Qurʾan 20:79.
28. Qurʾan 7:178.

may be held accountable. According to Wāṣil Ibn ʿAṭā, God is just, but it would not be just if God acted on behalf of people and then later held them accountable. At the same time, this means that people have to bear the consequences of their actions. The Muʿtazilites rejected the Umayyad concept, according to which divine praise and divine reproach reflect God's will rather than human actions.

The debate surrounding the question of whether people are responsible for their actions was politically motivated to start with in order to confirm the legitimization of the Umayyad rulers or to discredit them. Later, the topic was discussed within the framework of Islamic theology and labelled "the Science of Kalām."[29]

By outlining the historical background in more detail, I mainly wanted to illustrate the strong influence of political developments on the issue of divine action and Muslim free will.

The doctrine of determination prevailed primarily for political reasons because it allowed un-legitimized rulers to legitimize their claims to power.

On the other hand, the theological concern of the opponents of the Mu'tazila was to protect the omnipotence of God. Therefore, they held that there can be no other will besides the will of God. It is God alone who creates all actions. The Muʿtazila strictly rejected this idea but could not assert themselves. Only at the time of the Abbasid Caliph al-Maʾmun and his two successors al-Muʿtaṣim and al-Wāṯiq was their doctrine a state doctrine, which, however, the Caliph al-Mutawakkil immediately overturned and forbade. It was not exactly in the Caliphs' interest to speak of human freedom.

---

29. Another concern of the Mu'tazilites was to deny any negative divine traits. For example, they opposed the idea that God created evil, thus backing up their argument that human beings are the real "creators" of their own actions. This concern arose during their confrontation with the Mazda-worshippers who believed in one God for the good, and one God for the evil.

The Relationship between the Concept of God's Omnipotence and political Structures of Power

The premise that often prevails regarding the relationship between images of God and understandings of power is that either man's conception of his relationship to God in many ways has a decisive influence on man's attitude towards the sphere of power or, conversely, that man's attitude towards the sphere of power in many ways has a decisive influence on man's conception of his relationship to God. In other words, the fundamental question can be put this way: Does a particular image of God influence the way in which structures of power are formed in a society, or, on the contrary, do the structures of power in which people are socialized influence their conceptions of God? I do not see a one-way causality; rather, I see multi-layered interactions between images of God and power structures that make this a mutually interdependent relationship. Both influence and shape each other, whereby I see a preponderance in favor of the thesis that assumes that the image of God is influenced by the structures of power in each society.

However, since this is primarily an investigation from a theological perspective, I will focus here on the question of the influence of the image of God on attitudes toward power. I will do this in a general sense and of its influence on individual and social forms of access to institutionalized religion, as well as on the question of the susceptibility of images of God to political instrumentalization. For this purpose, I would like to contrast two different images of God within the idea of omnipotence. In doing so, it will be shown that the former image of God is easier to instrumentalize for the reproduction of absolute political structures of power than the latter image of God.

The Monological Image of God and the Authoritarian Society

According to the first image of God, which I would like to call "monological", God's omnipotence is explicated in such a way that God intervenes directly in the world to control and determine everything.

Nothing in the world happens without God determining the way in which it should occur. Omnipotence is understood here in terms of the classical Ashʿarite notion of omnipotence, as stated, for example, in al- Ghazālī (g. 1111).[30]

However, this understanding of omnipotence, which also extends to the absolute determination of human actions through God's omnipotence, is strongly rejected by contemporary Muslim philosophers of religion such as Ali Mabrouk (1961-2016) and Zacharia Ibrahim (1924-1976). Their concerns, however, are by no means to abandon the idea of an omnipotent God, for talk of God's omnipotence (arab. *qudra*) is firmly anchored in religious lore, and the name *al-Qādir* (the Almighty) is a crucial and essential characteristic of God often described in the Qur'an. Mabrouk's and Zacharias's concern is rather to redefine the concept of omnipotence, putting the ideal emphasis on the theological reclamation and restoration of man's freedom. According to Abu al-Ḥasan al-Ashʿarī (d. 936), the founder of the Ashʿarīte school of thought, "man has no power to execute what is willed; but the sole power to execute is possessed only by God."[31]

Ali Mabrouk sees especially in the Ashʿarīte dogma a reproduction of authoritarian structures that, in his view, had strengthened especially during the Umayyad (661-750) and Abbasid (750-1250) dynasties:

> "The Ašʿarites have collaborated, though unconsciously, in establishing an authoritarian historical epoch; and they have done so through their dogmatic design, subservient to an absolutism, be this based on God or on politics."[32]

---

30. Al- Ghāzalī. 2004. *Al-Iqtisād fī al-Iʿtiqad*. Beirut: Dar Kutub. p. 43.
31. Fahkr-al-Dīn al-Rāzī. 1979. *Muḥaṣṣal afkār al-Mutaqaddimīn waʾa-l-Mutaʾakhkhirīn min al-ʿulamāʾ wa-al-Ḥukamāʾ waʾl-Mutakallimīn*. Al-Qāhira: Maktabat al-Kullīyāt al-Azharīya, p. 194.
32. Mabrouk p. xx.

Mabrouk recalls here the Ash'-arite answer to the question: Is it God or man who brings forth man's actions? For the Ash'arites, the answer was clear: God. Man merely appropriates the actions created by God, but even this activity of appropriating actions is itself an action that God creates. Mabrouk, therefore, concludes that man appears here solely as an object of history. He is not truly free. His relation to God is not based on a relationship but on absolute submission.[33] Here Mabrouk notes:

> "Although the Aš'arites intended to preserve and uphold the absolute authority of God, beside which no proper existence of the world or of man receives attention, their dogmatic expositions led, even if unconsciously perhaps, to the affirmation of political claims to absoluteness in a world that is supposed to know no more real existence except that of the Absolute, whether as God or as despot. Therefore, from their beginnings, the Aš'arites were favored by rulers to legitimize their power."[34]

Mabrouk states that the theological discourse around such a conception of God draws a world that recognizes no other reference point besides God. This theological discourse sacrifices man and his actions in the world in order to preserve God's sovereignty. Mabrouk is skeptical of this notion of an absolutely authoritarian God. He recalls God's statement: "I was a hidden treasure and wanted to be known, that is why I created mankind."[35] Mabrouk describes these authoritarian structures as the product of a collective consciousness:

---

33. Ibid., 165.
34. Ibid., 166.
35. Ibid., 167.

"The Ašʿarite structures of an Absolute are a product of a historical epoch and a particular social situation and by no means represent a pure theological reflection on God as the Absolute. The Ašʿarite structure of thought thus provides the ideological underpinnings of a dictatorial state that can exist only if man is displaced."[36]

The Ashʿarite school, which sought to save and protect the freedom of God and thus rejected the freedom of man, made the mistake of playing off both liberties of God and man against each other. I would, however, like to show, based on the modern idea of freedom, that the revelation of God's freedom only works if man is granted his freedom. God's freedom is realized precisely if God gives freedom.

A Dialogical Image of God and the Modern Theology of Freedom

If one tries to appreciate the Qur'an in its entirety, one can say that it invites all people to a relationship with God. At the same time, from the Muslim perspective, it is God's self-revelation that effectively conveys the very presence of God to which it invites. The presence of God, to which the Qur'an wants to invite, is not only present through the revelation of the Qur'an, but shapes creation from the beginning. God, therefore, does not have to be added to the world in his revelation but embraces it from its first moment. Correspondingly, the Qur'an emphasizes that God is not outside the world but embraces it in his mercy (Q 7:156) and is at the same time closer to us humans than our jugular vein (Q 50:16).

According to the Qur'anic idea, God has chosen man in order to make him the offer to direct his life towards God. In doing so, God opened himself to man and became involved with him. And it

---

36. Ibid., 247.

is precisely this boundless and essential openness that constitutes the condition and basis of freedom, in which God gives man freedom in freedom and thereby enables him to self-determination. A God who gives man his own will and enables him to freedom is not a restrictive God who intervenes directly in the world to control and determine everything.

In his book "The Problem of Freedom" (*Mushkilat al-Hurriyya*), the Egyptian philosopher Zakaria Ibrāhīm (1924-1976) criticizes Spinoza, the Jewish philosopher of the *Deus sive Natura*, and asks several questions, which could lead us in our theological reflection: "What hinders us to accept that God himself wanted that free entities to exist; entities, which are equipped with a free will, a will not dependent upon the Divine will? Why can we not say that precisely because it is impossible that things exist, which are opposed to the Divine will, God would be able to create an entity, which is absolutely free?" (p. 136) Ibrāhīm continues further:

> "In fact, such autonomous power, which is enabled to emerge through God's free will, through the gift, which allows a will besides Him, could appear as restriction of the Divine omnipotence/ perfection. But could we not say that the absolute omnipotence of God would even become clearer in that sense that He creates powerful entities instead of incapable beings, which have no power nor a free will? How would we understand Divine power when He would only be able to create puppets? Is such an idea not an insult concerning our conviction of an omnipotent creator-God? And why don't we say that the more God grants autonomous power to His creation, the clearer His omnipotence appears? Because the magnitude of the gift-given points to the magnitude of the giver of the gift. Is our own freedom not the most honest evidence for God's absolute omnipotence?" (p. 137)

At the same time, Ibrāhīm sympathizes with the position of the Swiss philosopher Charles Secrétan (d. 1895), who sees God as absolute freedom, who is also free, concerning His own freedom. Secrétan raises the logical argument that God has decided, in absolute freedom, in favor of His omnipotence. This is a rather necessary operation because if God were perfect in His essence, it would be a contradiction because an absolutely perfect and giving God, a God that is perfect from eternity onwards, could not be less perfect and less omnipotent than a God, who had given Himself omnipotence by His free will. (Secrétan, p. 137) According to him, it is not logical to assume that God would be dependent on certain aspects of nature imposed onto Him; on the contrary, thinking God as absolutely free ultimately means that He would have chosen to be perfect and omnipotent by His freedom of choice. (p. 138) Secrétan sees creation as God's free choice, according to His free volition, and in turn, God grants His creation/humans autonomy by His freedom. God does not conduct this giving act to demonstrate His Divine glory and greatness but does so unconditionally and without a specific purpose. Otherwise, creation would not have been necessary and could not be understood as the result of God's free actions. Because God wants humans in an unconditioned manner, he grants them life. Therefore, God desires a human free of choice; he fulfills no purpose but the purpose of creation itself. (p. 138)

God is Freedom

As I said, the Ash'arite and Māturīdī schools have restrained the freedom of man to save the freedom of God. Both schools of theology agree that the major attribute of God is His *irāda* (will). Al-Taftzānī (d. 792/1390)–as well as several other scholars–subscribe to the thesis that *irāda* is independent of a causal motive. *Irāda,* according to him, is the motive of all motives within the Godhead itself. Nothing else is meant but absolute Divine freedom. Equally, Divine mercy must be understood in that tradition as an expression of the Divine will; against all objections, it must not be understood as a major attribute within the Divine as in classical theology and philosophical metaphysics. Thus, the usage of God as absolute freedom expresses the traditional Islamic understanding very well. We can summarize, therefore, that God destined Himself in His never-ending freedom to be merciful.

This is expressed in the aforementioned verse from the Qur'an: *kataba ʿalā nafsihi l-raḥmata*, "He has taken it upon Himself to be Merciful" (6:12) and *wa-mā arsalnāka illā raḥmatan li-l-ʿālamīn*, "And We did not send you except as a Mercy for the entire world" (21:107). Mercy was not an attribute of God before the world was created; mercy is not necessary in God by means of ontology, but mercy is elected by God as a major category within the Divine message, representing the center of the multi-faceted revealed teaching. Would it be otherwise, that God itself be represented in an ontological understanding as mercy, then the Qur'an would not need to mention that God has taken upon Himself to be merciful. And this is precisely the unchanging factor in God: His promise to be merciful. The human can rely on His mercy; he can find rest in God's mercy in life and death because he can completely trust in the Divine promise.

The God-Human-Relationship as an Expression of Freedom

The juxtaposition of God's freedom and human freedom, as the Ashʿarites and the Muʿtazilites have done, is based on a misunderstanding from the perspective of modern thinking on freedom. Mutahhari, therefore correctly criticizes both schools for sacrificing either God's freedom (the Muʿtazilites) or human freedom (the Ashʿarites).[37] Mutahhari proposes a third path, which assumes that God's freedom wants human freedom, and therefore, there is no competitive relationship between the two. In his book on the relationship

---

37. See Mutahhari p. 64, 72 und 102.

of destiny (*qadar*) to human freedom, he discusses the meaning of *qadar* in detail and shows that *qadar* does not mean determination at all but that God created the world according to laws so that causalities rule the world. God acts through these causalities; therefore, man always remains free to determine and be responsible for his actions.

Mutahhari cites various Qur'anic passages that seem to make contradictory statements: namely, a group of Qur'anic verses speaks of God as acting (e.g., Q pp. 95-95 in Mutahhari%%). Mutahhari, however, does not see any contradictions among these verses because, while it is correct to say that it is God who acts because He created the laws in the world according to which man acts, it is also correct to say that it is man who acts because the action comes about only when man makes use of and abides by the divine laws according to which the world was created.[38]

Modern thinking on freedom helps us, in my opinion, to go one step further, and that is by explicating the freedom of God, which the Ash'arites appreciated but did so at the expense of human freedom, in terms of modern thinking on freedom.

If man's freedom is to be preserved and protected, God will intervene in the world only in a way that does not violate that freedom. Therefore, God claims man's freedom in order to make freedom possible. It is man, in the first place, who realizes God's intention for love and mercy and transforms it into an experienceable reality here and now. Therein lies the highest dignification of man. He is God's partner, in the Qur'anic language *khalifa*, to make the divine intention a reality. Therefore, divine and human action must not be placed in a competitive relationship with each other. On the contrary, the more man is committed to the release of freedom, the more God's intention is realized. Man's commitment to the release of freedom is realized in

---

38. Mutahhari p. 95ff.

his action in the spirit of love and mercy. Both must therefore become an end in themselves of human action.

Conceiving the God-human relationship as a relationship of love and freedom influences the definition of it. Kierkegaard defines omnipotence as follows: "The greatest thing that can be done for a being at all, higher than anything one can do, is this: to make it free. Precisely to be able to do this, requires omnipotence."[39]

According to this conception, omnipotence is more than unlimited "being able to do everything logically possible". Klaus von Stosch formulates this:

> "Rightly understood omnipotence cannot be an all-dominating and controlling super-power, but is characterized precisely by the creation of beings who are themselves powerful and who, out of this granted power, can enter into a relationship of freedom with their Creator. But if the omnipotence is thought as power of bringing forth what is independent of oneself, which at the same time has the power to win this independent for itself, omnipotence can only be determined as love. For love alone is able to release power and to win it for itself in the release. Just a love which deserves unreserved trust, because it is just pure love. Only in love it can be thought that the devotion and self-sacrifice can be experienced as power, which positively surpasses every other power, because it is able to win for itself that which is independent of itself."[40]

Love is therefore, as Jürgen Werbick explains, "the power beyond which a greater, better power cannot be thought at all."[41] One can

---

39. See Kirkegard
40. See Klaus von Stosch
41. See Werbick, Jürgen. 2016. Gott verbindlich: Eine theologische Gotteslehre. Freiburg: Verlag Herder, p. 407.

precisely think nothing greater and nothing more powerful than the ability to give a counterpart complete autonomy.[42] This concept of power is dialogical, which sees God's activity in the world as based exclusively on the means of love. Here, no more spaces remain open for absolute claims to power in the sense of complete control of people by God or political authority.

God means absolute freedom; to think of Him as such points to creation as a self-perpetuating task. It goes back to the un-derivable will of God, who has decided in absolute freedom in favor of creation. This is *creatio ex nihilo*, often affirmed by theologians (*mutakallimūn*) and often rejected by philosophers (*falasifā*). Creation is the free acting of God, which is unbound of cause and effect. The relationship between man and God is, thus, not causal but determined by personal categories. God could have resolutely decided against a creation, as the German philosopher Lutker Lütkehaus contemplates, and nothing would have changed Him; nothing would have touched His omniscience and omnipotence.

God decided otherwise and, by creating humans, entrusts them with high expectations, namely, the acceptance of God's invitation. The acceptance of His love and mercy manifests in the willingness to become thankful for creation, love, and mercy. If the goal of creation is to find freely devoted co-lovers—*fa-sawfa yaʾti llāhu bi-qawmin yuḥibbuhum wa-yuḥibbūnahu*, 'He [God] will bring a people He loves and who will love him' (5:54) --, then one could easily say that the ultimate goal of creation is the realization of freedom. Only the affirmation of freedom allows/enables freedom. Therefore, God is freedom. God's original will is a will for openness and, thereby, for freedom. If unlimited general openness is the condition of autonomy, then the destination of autonomy is

---

42. See T. Pröpper, Art. Allmacht Gottes. In: LThK 1 (31993), 412-417, 416: Since nothing greater is conceivable than a love that wants other freedom and responds to their killing negation in their favor without being destroyed, only such love can be considered true omnipotence.

the affirmation of freedom, and for this reason, the content of freedom can only be freedom.

Mankind is a medium to realize God's love and mercy by voluntary acting. God and mankind are co-workers to realize both. The completeness of a human being is correlated to God's working through him. God's plans are more realized by the personal increase in fulfilling God's will. Divine intentions become real if persons are ready to act in a way of love. The surplus of this model is that there is a proportional increase of divine and human freedom in their immanent acting. The release of freedom through God is an end in itself. The reason is yet alone the free decision of God to create, allow, and respect another form of freedom. The one who has decided to release freedom will not use measures to restrict the freedom of the other.

Without true freedom, honest love cannot exist, *yuḥibbuhum wa-yuḥibbūnahu*, 'He loves and who will love him' (5:54). God starts with Himself, to direct the attention to His self-commitment to love. Now, the more the human invests in actualizing freedom, the more the original intentions of God are realized. The commitment of the human for the release of freedom manifests in his very actions by means of love and mercy. Both love and mercy must become the sole purpose of human actions.

To find co-lovers is predetermined by the free agreement of the human, and, thus, the agreement to freedom. When God sends His prophets and messages at certain points in time, it's only because he wants to win over humans. Therefore, the Qur'an speaks of *da'wa*, invitation. This invitation can only be accepted in freedom as the emerging relationship is governed by love: *yuḥibbuhum wa-yuḥibbūnahu*, 'He loves and who will love him' (5:54). If the freedom of the human is vouchsafed and protected, God will only interfere in the unfolding of events without touching this freedom. It could even be said that God uses the freedom of mankind to actualize freedom because it is the humans, first of all, who realize God's intentions for love and mercy and who turn abstract concepts into experienceable categories. This is the highest honor of mankind. He is the partner of God, in Qur'anic dictum *khalīfa*, 'surrogate' or 'substitute.' It is the surrogate partner of God who actualizes the Divine intentions. Therefore, the human is the object of love and the pledge of love for others. He himself is authorized, instructed to mete out love and mercy to others and to give a face to Divine action. These two acts of freedom—the acting of the human as surrogate and the acting of God—are two sides of one coin and should not be understood by means of competition.

The believer is a servant of God because he is a medium for God's intentions. God is mainly acting in our world through human beings, and for this reason, we can say, in a certain way, that God 'needs' humans to realize his intentions of love and mercy. But God's 'dependency' on mankind is not a sign of weakness because God is mercy in himself even if it is not realized in our world. God is totally merciful. God does not depend on mankind in an ontological way. He decided freely for this kind of interaction with the world. The companion Abu Huraira reports having heard Muhammad, the Prophet, tell the following story:

> Verily, God, the Exalted and Glorious, would say on the Day of Resurrection: O son of Adam, I was sick, but you did not visit Me. He would say: O my Lord; how could I visit You whereas you are the Lord of the worlds? Thereupon He would say: Didn't you know that such and such servant of Mine was sick, but you did not visit him and were you not aware of this that if you had visited him, you would have found Me by him? O son of Adam, I asked food from you, but you did not feed Me. He would say: My Lord, how could I feed you whereas you are the Lord of the worlds? He said: Didn't you know that such and such servant of Mine asked food from you, but you did not feed him, and were you not aware that if

you had fed him you would have found him by My side? (The Lord would again say:) O son of Adam, I asked drink from you but you did not provide Me. He would say: My Lord, how could I provide you whereas you are the Lord of the worlds? Thereupon He would say: Such and such of servant of Mine asked you for a drink but you did not provide him, and had you provided him drink you would have found him near Me."[43]

A very similar story can be found in Matthew's Gospel, chapter 25: "Whatever you did for one of the least of these brothers and sisters of mine, you did for me." God is present when a human needs Him. Every human testimony of merciful love to a fellow creature is an answer to God's love. Spirituality enables a human being to see God's merciful face in the face of every human being and to serve God by serving every fellow creature. Every simple act of mercy is a manifestation of God. Where mercy is, there is God. A mother embracing her child, a smile, a sign of goodness, love, and mercy: all of them reveal God's mercy and call for the experiencing of God. In every act of mercy, finally, God is present.

Therefore, the concept of mercy is a living religious act. Living in increasing freedom is the assumption for an increasing realization of God's intentions of love and mercy through my words and acts. A merciful life is the essence of spirituality and, at the same time, the norm of spirituality.

---

43. Muslim ibn al-Ḥajjā, *Saḥīḥ Muslim*, Ḥadīth No. 2569.

ALSO FROM
SacraSage Press...

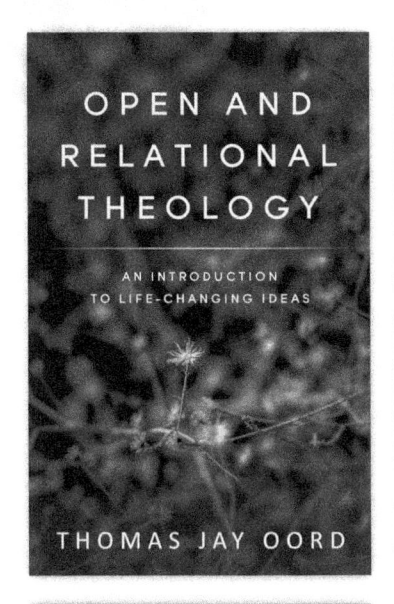

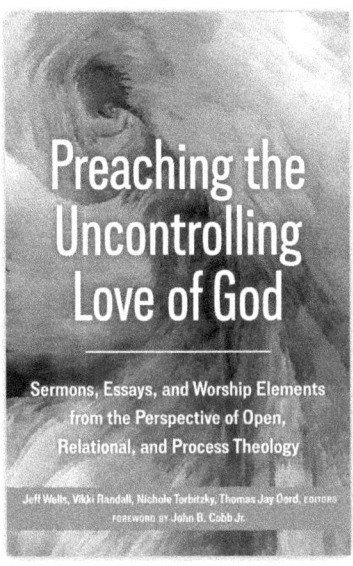

OPEN AND RELATIONAL THEOLOGY
AN INTRODUCTION TO LIFE-CHANGING IDEAS
THOMAS JAY OORD

Preaching the Uncontrolling Love of God
Sermons, Essays, and Worship Elements from the Perspective of Open, Relational, and Process Theology
Jeff Wells, Vikki Randall, Nichole Torbitzky, Thomas Jay Oord, EDITORS
FOREWORD BY John B. Cobb Jr.

JOHN B. COBB, JR.
SELECTED WRITINGS FROM A CHRISTIAN THEOLOGIAN
Tripp Fuller and Wm Andrew Schwartz, eds.

OPEN AND RELATIONAL LEADERSHIP
Leading with Love
Roland Hearn, Sheri D. Kling, & Thomas Jay Oord, EDITORS

SACRASAGEPRESS.COM